Natural History of Silence

Natural History of Silence

JÉRÔME SUEUR

Translated by Helen Morrison

polity

First published in French as *Histoire naturelle du silence* © Actes Sud, 2023

This English edition © Polity Press, 2025

This book is supported by the Institut français (Royaume-Uni) as part of the Burgess programme.

Polity Press
65 Bridge Street
Cambridge CB2 1UR, UK

Polity Press
111 River Street
Hoboken, NJ 07030, USA

All rights reserved. Except for the quotation of short passages for the purpose of criticism and review, no part of this publication may be reproduced, stored in a retrieval system or transmitted, in any form or by any means, electronic, mechanical, photocopying, recording or otherwise, without the prior permission of the publisher.

ISBN-13: 978-1-5095-6401-9 – hardback
ISBN-13: 978-1-5095-6402-6 – paperback

A catalogue record for this book is available from the British Library.

Library of Congress Control Number: 2024937922

Typeset in 11 on 14pt Warnock Pro
by Cheshire Typesetting Ltd, Cuddington, Cheshire
Printed and bound by CPI Group (UK) Ltd, Croydon, CR0 4YY

The publisher has used its best endeavours to ensure that the URLs for external websites referred to in this book are correct and active at the time of going to press. However, the publisher has no responsibility for the websites and can make no guarantee that a site will remain live or that the content is or will remain appropriate.

Every effort has been made to trace all copyright holders, but if any have been overlooked the publisher will be pleased to include any necessary credits in any subsequent reprint or edition.

For further information on Polity, visit our website:
politybooks.com

Contents

Acknowledgements vii
Foreword by Gilles Boeuf ix

1. In the Alps — 1
2. The essence of sound — 5
3. In the tropics — 19
4. The nature of sounds — 27
5. In the heart of the Jura — 42
6. The enemy — 45
7. In the laboratory — 57
8. Absolute — 60
9. Natural — 68
10. Pleyel — 77
11. Music! — 81
12. Ourselves and others — 91
13. To hear or not to hear — 96
14. At the museum — 107
15. Past — 113

16	Hiding	124
17	Solar days	141
18	Romantic	145
19	Together	155
20	Sharing	164
21	Battles	169
22	Where?	178
23	Great silences	185
24	Silence, lockdown!	192
25	Preserving silence	198

Conclusion	206
Notes	208

Acknowledgements

Thanks to...

inspiring and enlightening conversations with Dominique Dupuy;

time spent exploring natural history and acoustics in the company of Julien Barlet, Adèle de Baudouin, Pablo Bolaños, Camille Desjonquères, Manon Ducrettet, Pierre-Michel Forget, Amandine Gasc, Philippe Gaucher, Elie Grinfeder, Sylvain Haupert, Laurent Lellouch, Félix Michaud, Sarah Obaid, Stéphane Puissant, Marie-Pierre Reynet, Frédéric Sèbe, Simon Targowla, Juan Sebastian Ulloa;

careful and thoughtful re-readings by Thierry Aubin, Laure Belmont, Bernie Krause, Sabrina Krief, André Nel, Emmanuelle Vin;

messages of support, advice and friendship from Stéphane Durand;

little notebooks made of paper and silence given to me by Caroline, Chloé and Julia;

... I have successfully completed this silent little exploration.

Many, many thanks to you all!

Foreword

What a book!!

Natural history of silence . . . What a wonderful title . . . Is nature sometimes silent? Yes, but not very often! In 2011, at the Muséum national d'histoire naturelle in Paris, Jérôme Sueur introduced me to someone who was subsequently to become a friend – the extraordinary American bioacoustician Bernie Krause, who had just published *The Great Animal Orchestra*. Bernie was in Paris to introduce the exhibition of the same name at the Fondation Cartier. This exhibition would make history and would be a way of saving Bernie's sound recordings lost during the great fire in California.

Since the end of the 1960s, Bernie Krause, frequently cited by the author in his book, has been a major pioneer in the study of the sounds of nature, contributing to the development of a new discipline in the United States – bioacoustics. Together, he and Jérôme initiated me into 'the sounds of nature' . . . Even if, ever since the dawn of time, humans – hunters and gatherers and then farmers and stockbreeders – have listened to nature, scientific and technological approaches have been slow to take off and, until very recently, these sounds have been scientifically little exploited. During the first half of the twentieth century, sounds were recorded using the phonograph, and then, gradually, new technological developments began to appear, largely thanks to the boom in electronics. Oscilloscopes, acoustic cameras, microphones and hydrophones ever more finely tuned (and often used to record whale 'songs') allowed increasingly sophisticated approaches and prepared the ground for the expansion of this new discipline.

Most recent progress concerns the impact of anthropogenic noise (the sound of human activities or the 'anthropophony') on the living and examines the relationships between humans, 'non-humans' and their acoustic environment, often referred to as a 'soundscape'. New research also focuses on a non-invasive technique for measuring biodiversity (for certain species of frog, for example, which are indistinguishable in appearance but which produce totally different sounds), leading to a new discipline, ecoacoustics, born just a few years ago in France at the Muséum national d'histoire naturelle.

In his book, Jérôme Sueur writes: 'Omnipresent outside, sound also rumbles continuously inside us. It enters through our ears and does not re-emerge, it travels effortlessly through our bodies, it reaches our organs, touches our unborn children. Our bodies are themselves a source of sound, pulsing constantly with the beating of our hearts, grinding in our sleep, creaking as our joints stretch and gurgling with gastric rumblings when we are seized by hunger.

At each moment, day and night, we are therefore both the target and the source of these sound arrows. All we need to do in order to tune into this omnipresent sound is to close our eyes, concentrate for a few seconds, and analyse the acoustic landscape that is playing out all around us. Voices, music, bodies, plants, winds, rains, storms and objects send or re-send the sounds which continuously bombard all of us, all the time, and which rarely come in isolation but are often mixed with others.'

This book is therefore a wonderful incitement to listen to all the 'soundscapes' which surround us. The author sets himself the task of describing to us, sometimes with a great deal of poetry and always with a solid technical and scientific base, a profusion of species and environments, whether mainland or oceanic, terrestrial or aquatic. Are we capable of detecting these sounds and understanding them? We have a very clear memory of the sights and smells of our childhood but does the same apply to sounds? It is true that we have lost a good deal in terms of our abilities to perceive our immediate environments, our senses dulled by lives which are so very different and so cut off from the nature in which we were immersed not so very long ago. We have only to look, for example, at Australian Aborigines who are capable of hearing a lizard burrowing in the desert sand, an essential capacity for survival in such hostile environments.

'Noise, the enemy of silence, makes no attempt to disguise itself. It is an insidious and large-scale enemy which makes itself heard at all times and in all circumstances . . .' And this situation triggers a great many harmful effects and debilitating conditions in humans, in spite of the fact that the vast majority of noises are created by strictly human activities (anthropophony). 'Man does not like noise but likes to make noise.' Just listen to the sarabands of jet-skis along our shores or on our lakes during the summer! If I make noise, then I exist! Is silence therefore 'a sound which does not make a noise'? What a lovely definition, formulated by a nursery school child!

What then must be done to put a stop to these endless cacophonies of anthropophony? A major lockdown such as we have recently experienced with a more than 99 per cent drop in noise pollution in areas close to airports? Evidence clearly indicates that overflights represent the most significant source of noise pollution in certain uninhabited 'wilderness' areas. Or should we go in search of that zone of silence set up by the ONF around the Chartreuse monastery in the Alps, where it is forbidden to . . . make any noise? Vladimir Nabokov tells us that silence is multiple and full of secrets, but it is by no means a void, an emptiness ... So, as in Saint-Martin-du-Canigou, that splendid abbey in the Catalan region of the Pyrenees with those sculpted monks in the cloisters, should we too make our mouths smaller and our ears bigger?

Indeed, alongside the omnipresent pollution of our civilizations, of chemical, physical (including radioactive) and biological (with species distributed all over the world) contaminations, should we also include light and sound pollution? The sounds produced by living organisms (biophony) have been of such vital importance since the origins of life, and these, along with those of geophony (the sounds of the physical world such as volcanos, thunder, waves ...), have shaped life as we know it. And they have often been a source of inspiration for our music ... So, as in that wonderful song by Paul Simon and Art Garfunkel, let us learn to listen to *The Sound of Silence* ...

Bergerac, 14 September 2022

GILLES BOEUF
Professor at the Sorbonne University,
former president of the Muséum national
d'histoire naturelle, visiting professor at the
Collège de France

1

In the Alps

It is an easy drive from Saint-Pierre-de-Chartreuse down to the flat plains of the Dauphiné region. This former track leading to the Chartreuse monastery is now a tranquil little mountain road, winding gently downhill, with only a few sharp bends to negotiate. There is a single narrow section under overhanging rocks where those heading cheerfully uphill find themselves almost rubbing shoulders with the unhappy travellers on their way back down.

On the occasion in question, we were ourselves part of the less fortunate group, heading back down to the plain, and, worse still, to the straight lines and heavy traffic of the main roads leading towards the flat and dreary Parisian basin.

Feeling the need for fresh air, snowy expanses and high, empty landscapes, we had decided to take a family break in the Chartreuse region, the nearest mountain range accessible from the western lowlands and one with a name that conjured up all the mystery of a place cut off from the rest of the world.

In that year, and those that followed, we would accumulate many memories on the slopes of these snowy mountains. That first week turned out to be a rather hectic one. Wonderful moments of noisy games in the virgin snow, far from the smoothly ploughed slopes, were interspersed with a number of minor family catastrophes: the car with its alarmingly slippery tyres getting stuck in the ice and snow, our three-year-old daughter falling head (and teeth) first down the steep staircase of a former barn now cosily converted and rented out on a weekly basis by an unerringly kind couple, and a nasty stomach bug passed from children to parents and vice versa, through some strange form of family altruism.

It was during this short stay – a time in which everything felt strangely compressed, punctuated with the to-ing and fro-ing of medical visits and often confined within the cosy though rather small chalet, our feet snug in thick new socks – that I found myself with an unexpected opportunity to make a brief escape into the surrounding pine forest.

Mountains have almost always scared me with their sheer mass and the threat of landslips or avalanches weighing heavily on the frail shoulders of my pallid city-dwelling self. Until then, I had never spent much time on rock faces or on snowy slopes. Only a handful of winter trips where I had skied – as people did thirty years ago, and still do today – a bit mindlessly, or at least in a tight group and always at high speed, without paying much attention to either the distant peaks or, nearer to hand, the animal and plant lives which might survive among the pylons and the ski-lifts. A few summer trips too, in the Pyrenees, trying to track down a mysterious frog on the slopes of Mount Canigou, or in the Swiss Alps, on that occasion in quest of an almost equally mysterious red cicada. My perception of the mountains was a very blinkered one, a vision which did not extend much beyond what could be seen through a ski mask or a cheap pair of goggles purchased in a large Paris store in the section tucked between horse-riding and aqua-gym. A stranger in the Chartreuse mountains, this escape from the chalet thanks to an enforced siesta for the rest of the family, still suffering the effects of the stomach bug, turned out to be a real moment of discovery for me.

I got dressed – even perhaps, like a true Parisian, overdressed – and quickly thrust my feet into a pair of snowshoes, grabbing the poles thoughtfully provided by the chalet owners. Under a grey but luminous sky, I took the first path to the right of the chalet, heading up the slope and into trees, dark against the snow.

In the course of this very short walk, I quickly realized that something was happening, or rather, not happening. True, I had escaped from a house full to the brim with activity and loud voices, but suddenly and without any prior expectation on my part, I found myself stepping into a completely different sound environment.

Advancing slowly along the snowy track, I ventured a short way from the path, carefully memorizing a few visual markers so as to avoid getting lost. As I walked, I could feel the crisp crunch of my snowshoes and poles on the hard snow, the rustle of my waterproofs and the rasp of my breath inside my scarf.

It was only when I stopped, after a few hundred metres, that I finally realized exactly what was happening.

Deep in the Chartreuse mountain range, far from the laboratory, far from the bustle of Paris life, nature was more alive, colder and more vibrant than ever before. Stripped of human noises, it presented itself to the passing hiker in its raw, unadorned state. In the cold air, there was only the flutter of a coal tit in search of something to eat and the muffled slither of a slab of snow sliding from a branch and falling slowly to the ground, leaving no trace of its presence.

It was there, at the end of that very short walk, standing alone and motionless in the snow, cut off from the relentless pace of time, that finally, for the very first time, I experienced silence in a natural world teeming with life.

And so, during the drive home, in the course of which my eye would be caught by a curious sign at the side of the road,

I resolved that, from then on, I would set myself the task of trying to listen to what no one else was listening to, to listen to what was supposedly emptiness, while others concentrated their attention on what was ostensibly full.

2

The essence of sound

In the space of just a short walk in my snowshoes, I had experienced the deep silence of a snowbound mountain landscape. Was this therefore what silence meant? A moment of solitude and of peace in a natural environment encased in ice and cold? Was silence an acoustic stillness where only a few flakes of sound still drifted past – a rustling of feathers, the slither of snow falling from branches? Was silence an absence of sounds and, as a result, a lack of information emanating from the surrounding landscape?

Yet, if this is indeed the case, how can we set about identifying an absence, a sort of emptiness? How can we define this antimatter, silence, without turning our attention to matter, in the form of sound? In order to understand silence, we must necessarily be familiar with sound. Who or what exactly is sound? What is this quivering yet formless creature which constantly makes its presence felt, even as we sleep, in the circumvolutions of our outer ears, tapping softly against our eardrums, gently stirring the stapes, the malleus and the incus in our inner ears, circling through the spirals of our cochlea, travelling along our nerves like a train advancing on its tracks, and finally awakening the neurones in our brains?

According to the laws of physics, sound is a modification of the pressure or density of a gas, fluid or solid caused by the endogenous or exogenous vibration of an object. Regardless of what that object is – a piano, a toaster, a copper beech or a whale – sound travels through air, water, vegetable or mineral matter. Without its medium, sound is nothing. In fact, sound is an integral part of the medium through which it is propagated: sound is air, water, plant or pebble and has been there since gases, liquids or solids first existed on earth. If sound fades with distance, bounces back and is diffracted by obstacles, it can also pass from one medium to another, from air to water, from water to rock, from rock to plants and from plants to air. Sound knows no frontiers; it disperses, permeates and then spreads out in all directions. All routes are possible as long as sound retains sufficient energy and the matter it travels through is capable of distortion.

Today, as I write, everything around me is vibrating in an atmosphere of hypersensitivity; the blue tit on the cherry tree in the garden, the radio in the kitchen, the neighbour's cat. Far away from me, sound is also vibrating. At exactly the same moment, sound is travelling to and fro in the humidity of tropical forests, in the frozen wastes of taigas, in the arid expanses of deserts. It plunges into the water of streams, lakes, rivers, ponds, seas and oceans, it passes through flowers, shoots, buds, fruit, leaves, trunks and branches and it travels through rocky ground, across sandy beaches and deep into the earth's crust.

Omnipresent outside, sound also rumbles continuously inside us. It enters through our ears and does not re-emerge, it travels effortlessly through our bodies, it reaches our organs, touches our unborn children. Our bodies are themselves a source of sound, pulsing constantly with the beating of our hearts, grinding in our sleep, creaking as our joints stretch and gurgling with gastric rumblings when we are seized by hunger.

At each moment, day and night, we are therefore both the target and the source of these sound arrows. All we need to do in order to tune into this omnipresent sound is to close our eyes, concentrate for a few seconds, and analyse the acoustic landscape that is playing out all around us. Voices, music, bodies, plants, winds, rains, storms and objects send or re-send the sounds which continuously bombard all of us, all the time, and which rarely come in isolation but are often mixed with others.

Sound is an essential element of our lives both inside and outside the womb, and a key to our survival. Sound in the form of the spoken word is the fundamental basis of our family and social relationships and keeps us constantly informed about the state of our environment and any changes to it. The framework of an immense network which connects and informs living creatures, sound is also a source of distraction, of relaxation. It alerts us, stimulates us and sometimes controls or irritates us. Sound penetrates our bodies for better as well as for worse.

In the air, sound is the relatively regular and relatively complex alternation of the longitudinal compressions and dilations of atmospheric particles. These particles oscillate around their position, never moving much further away than a few dozen nanometres. This small and very precise movement gives rise to an important phenomenon: the nano-oscillations of particles are transmitted from one to another in such a way that the alternating compression-dilation is capable of being transmitted over long distances, sometimes as much as several kilometres. The movements of the particles are small and weak, but the sound wave is big and powerful and the differences in pressure which occur can have a dramatic effect on us. How strange that we are incapable of seeing sound even though it is sometimes so intense as to be painful. In order to do that, we are obliged to resort to a little help from sensitive receptors in the form of microphones, accelerometers, laser vibrometers and mathematical manipulations capable of converting sound into image.

The physical description of a sound wave is made up of four main dimensions: amplitude, duration, frequency and phase. Amplitude is the strength, pressure, energy, power and intensity of the sound. All these terms from mechanical physics are linked to each other by variables of acceleration, mass, surface, density, celerity, impedance and time. Beyond the underlying mathematics, which are in fact relatively straightforward, it is simply a matter of remembering that the greater the amplitude of a sound, the more that sound distorts its medium of transport. The trumpeting of an African elephant displaces air particles to a greater extent than do the wingbeats of the mosquito buzzing around its ears.

The second dimension, a purely temporal one, is easier to grasp. A sound is not an indefinite event. It has a beginning and an end, a duration. While each sound contains its own history, made up of complex events of transduction, diffusion, dispersal, propagation, refraction, reflection and diffraction, sound is essentially transient, an event of the moment. The birth of a sound is relatively easy to determine given that it corresponds to the beginning of the vibration which occurs when the particles of the medium pass from a state of rest to a state of activity. This process is usually a rapid one, marked by a clear increase in amplitude. The death of a sound, on the other hand, is more difficult to pin down. Sound can often take a certain time to fade completely. The length of time required for a sound to die depends first of all on the physical absorption properties of its source and, in particular, its mass and elasticity. A resonating object such as a church bell takes longer to stop vibrating than a sound which is more spontaneously produced, like the snapping of fingers. The duration of a sound also, and even more importantly, depends on the inherent physical properties of the medium, such as its volumetric mass and impedance, and the extent to which the physical space is encumbered by the presence of other objects which can reflect the sound, creating echoes, or, on the contrary, absorbing and stopping it.

Subtle, discreet, hidden behind the broad shield of temporal variations and amplitude, phase nevertheless plays an essential role in the production, propagation and reception of sound. Phase is a temporal property which is a little more difficult to grasp since it is expressed in an unfamiliar unit, the radian, and with the golden number of π. Phase is used to define periodic sounds, or in other words, sounds which have repeated or cyclical time patterns. It is a way of describing position and indicates the location of the wave within the wave cycle which is circular in form.

Finally, frequency, perhaps the best-known aspect of sound, corresponds to the number of cycles travelled by a sound wave in a second, a number expressed in hertz (Hz). The greater the number of cycles, the higher the sound, and conversely. The sounds which surround us are very rarely made up of a single frequency but are more often a whole range of sounds covering a wide spectrum of frequencies, ranging from low frequencies of just a few hertz to very high frequencies measuring several thousand hertz. Sounds inaudible to humans are referred to as infrasounds when frequencies are lower than 20 hertz and as ultrasounds when they are in excess of 20,000 hertz.

Since a musical metaphor is unavoidable when it comes to describing sound, it is possible to see amplitude in terms of nuances such as *pianissimo, forte, fortissimo*, duration in the form of notes, quavers, quarter notes, whole notes, and frequency in terms of pitch – C, D, E. Only phase, eternally forgotten, does not seem to have any equivalent in the western system of musical notation, even if it is an important factor in the craftsmanship of instruments and in the engineering behind sound recording and reproduction.

Amplitude, duration, frequency and phase are not independent properties – amplitude is measured in a predefined temporal window, frequency is the opposite of a temporal period, duration is a specific time, and phase is a characteristic of both amplitude and time. Time is therefore the fundamental dimension of sound.

Hearing means listening to the passing of time.

Soft or violent, short or prolonged, low or high-pitched, sound does not come from nowhere but emerges from a vibrating object.

Green tree frogs (*Hyla arborea*) are endearing-looking frogs which conjure up an image of a plump rounded body, a broad grin at the water's edge, a fly trapped like a sandwich in its mouth and skin the colour of a Granny Smith apple. The tree frog is also known for its capacity to leap over water lilies the size of flying saucers and for its croaking sounds, which are as insistent as they are incomprehensible.

Straight out of the pages of a fairy tale, the little green frog with sticky toe pads occupies a privileged place in our imaginations. But if the tree frog croaks loudly in our bedtime stories, few of us venture out at night to listen to it in the ditches of a waterlogged lane or around the edges of a pond. True, it requires a certain amount of courage to switch off our screens and head out into the darkness, dirtying our boots in muddy water. And yet it is an experience which is both moving and rewarding. We should make the effort, spend some time searching in the long grass, on stones or in damp earth in quest of this little animal, crouched like a cat ready for its nap, until finally we find it, fully concentrated on its nightly task of calling and calling, again and again, its throat swollen almost to bursting point as it proclaims its romantic longings to the stars turning far above its tiny, fragile head.

The male tree frog is a tireless singer. Like all vertebrates, its song relies on the vibration of delicate membranes attached to its larynx, the equivalent of our vocal cords. At the start of the process, the frog takes a breath in, then, contracting its abdominal muscles, it expels the air from its lungs towards its mouth. The air passes over the larynx and forces the vocal cords to vibrate. While most terrestrial singing animals take a breath between two bouts of song, the tree frog functions in a closed circuit. The air in the lungs travels across the larynx and the vocal cords, passes over the glottis and enters the mouth cavity, kept firmly closed by the male frog, his jaws clenched and nostrils tightly sealed. Air then travels back in the opposite direction towards the lungs and this process is constantly repeated. This closed ventilation system allows the tree frog to sing for a long period without needing to take in air, therefore avoiding the tiring movements of external respiration.[1]

The tree frog therefore never deflates during the mating call, with air alternately dilating the lungs and the mouth. The roof of the mouth is pierced ventrally by two small openings leading to a delicate, flexible membrane forming the throat. Under the pressure of air coming from the lungs, this membrane, the vocal sac, swells up like a balloon. Sporting this curious double chin, the frog takes on a strangely aristocratic look. Indeed, the vocal sac plays a crucial role in sound production since it enhances amplification by facilitating the transfer of vibrations from the frog's body to the outside air, improves tone by concentrating the sound energy on just a few specific frequencies and helps acoustic diffusion by projecting the sound in all directions. Without the vocal sac, the sound produced by the tree frog would be distorted, fainter, more difficult to locate and probably less agreeable to listen to along the edges of a lane.

The sac swells up and vibrates. Our eyes are sadly not quick enough but it is almost possible to see the vibrations on the surface of the taut membrane, on the interface between the amphibian body and the air. This is the origin of the airborne sound, the sound wave which reaches our ears. If, by chance, the tree frog is immersed in water, the sound can also travel from the vocal sac to the water and at that point a regular series of little ripples form around it in concentric circles. Sound becomes visible and radiates out from the frog.

Seeing sound in the white throat of a tree frog sitting in a puddle gives us an opportunity to try to understand the mechanics and the rationale of an animal sound. The frog makes throaty sounds, since it is the throat that is doing the work here. It distorts its body in order to distort the air, water or ground around it and, for a certain period, takes control of all of this. Singing is a competitive sport.

For the croaking to make sense, for it to be the outcome of an evolutionary process, it must of course be noticed, detected, recognized, identified and localized and it must have a function other than that of simply making the frog visible to passing predators. There must be a very good reason behind this behaviour. And it is a simple one: the drive to reproduce, to pass on its genes to another generation. Like almost all animals, the tree frog becomes vocal when love is in the air, when it is time to find a partner. The male sends out a communication signal which contains various different elements of information, essentially for the benefit of any nearby females. That guttural croak divulges information about identity: 'I am a green tree frog'; gender: 'I am a male'; current state: 'I am ready to reproduce'; location: 'I am here'; and quality: 'I swear that with me you will have the most beautiful tadpoles.' This communication is an essential element in the tree frog's life: the croaking is the keystone of its life cycle. Removing the sound would result in the loss of the species.

Sound exists in its own right but it takes on a value, a behavioural, social or ecological purpose, when it is detected and interpreted by a living creature possessing a sense of hearing and an integral nervous system capable of reading and interpreting information coded in the properties of amplitude, duration, frequency and phase. The first stage in the process of hearing is the transfer of sound, which must travel from the outside to the inside of the body, whether human, pink dolphin or tree frog. In this particular case, there is a physical problem in that air offers little resistance to sound, or in other words, the impedance of air is relatively weak, whereas the biological tissue of the frog, essentially made up of water and fatty matter, offers a certain amount of resistance to sound and therefore a high level of impedance. The transition from one to the other is no easy matter. One solution to facilitate transmission from outside to inside is to diminish the impedance of the receiving body, notably by reducing the thickness of the external tissues as much as possible. The tree frog has a very fine membrane called a tympanum, behind which is concealed an air-filled cavity. Delicate, light and flexible, the tympanum receives the sound vibrations from the air, thereby allowing sound to enter.

In frogs, as in most animal species, the hearing process involves a series of mechanical and physiological stages. Air is distorted and transformed into movements of the tympanum which are then transmitted to the columella, an ossicle equivalent to our stapes bone, and this in turn connects with the oval window of the cochlea in the inner ear. Mechanical vibrations are then transformed into electrical impulses, the basis of nerve signals, in a cluster of sensory neurones which together form the auditory nerve. The auditory nerve projects into the brain, notably in a nucleus called the *torus semicircularis*, which processes information coded within the parameters of time, amplitude, frequency and phase. The frog on the receiving end of the song is therefore capable of detecting, identifying, localizing and decoding the message emitted by the croaking frog, a process which is fundamental to any system of communication and therefore of socialization.

But sound does not always pass through the main tympanic entrance. It can also be picked up by other parts of the body and transmitted to the brain. The American green tree frog (*Dryophytes cinereus*), cousin of the European green tree frog, uses its lungs as well as its ears to listen to other frogs of the same species. The sound reaches the tympanum through their external surface via a direct route and travels to their internal surface by a roundabout, visceral one. Sound can in fact pass through the lungs, the glottis, the mouth or the Eustachian tubes in order to make the internal surface of the tympanums vibrate. The Gardiner's Seychelles frog (*Sechellophryne gardineri*), one of the smallest amphibians in the world, has neither external nor internal ears and therefore no tympanum or columella. At first sight, therefore, it should not be able to hear. And yet, it sings. Experiments conducted on the idyllic island of Silhouette and morpho-anatomical analyses have shown that it reacted strongly to the songs of its own species and that sound was clearly finding another pathway. In the case of this frog, sound is transmitted through the mouth cavity, which acts as a resonator. The waves then travel through the jaw bones and reach the inner ear.[2]

In this way, certain frogs hear with their bodies, their lungs or their mouths. Animals have multiple means of receiving or emitting sound. Flies and mosquitoes hear with their antennae, which are also their nose, cicadas broadcast their song in the blazing heat of the Provençal garrigue with the aid of their tymbals, fish hear thanks to their swim bladder which acts as a ballast for vertical navigation, kangaroo rats chat by tapping their feet and crustaceans listen with the help of their sensilla, sensory hairlike structures covering their bodies. If we are to enter the realm of the acoustic lives of animals, we need essentially to set aside everything associated with the processes we ourselves use for emitting or receiving sound and avoid any comparison between our anatomy, our vocal capacities and our auditory properties and those of the animals around us. Sound is not necessarily a voice, and ears are not necessarily located on the head.

But what do frogs hear? Without going into the neurobiological details, frogs, like other animals, do not hear in the way we do and it is hard for us to imagine exactly what their perception of sound is like. The auditory capacities of frogs may appear more restricted given that their frequential sensitivity, that is to say the frequencies they are most likely to pick up, is very often limited to a window corresponding to the frequencies of their song. This means that there is some form of connection between the frequencies emitted and the frequencies picked up which effectively excludes any sounds which are of no interest from a survival point of view. The ear, from the tympanum to the cerebral nuclei, functions partly as a series of filters only permitting the transmission of those frequencies which carry information and enable a female frog to react to the declarations made by the emitter of the sounds, for example those revealing his identity, such as 'I am a green tree frog'. What applies for frequencies also applies to the time structure of the signals in question. The neurones adjacent to the ear and the central neurones of the brain only become active if the rhythm of any vocalizations, or of the impulses which constitute these, corresponds to a recognized rate of repetition, for example thirty beats per second. In this way frequential and temporal filters play a role in decoding the information concealed within the frog's croaking.

Each frog, each species, but also each individual therefore perceives their surrounding environment in their own way, and in a way which is very different way from our own, effectively ruling out any generalization based on our own acoustic perception and, in consequence, any anthropomorphism or anthropocentrism.

Sound is a universal mechanical wave which travels through space without leaving any trace but which carries information and sensations unique to each living creature. Weak in terms of the movements of its particles, scarcely visible, the sound wave has a fundamental effect on the tree frog and, of course, on all species relying on sound. The tree frog uses sound in the reproductive cycle in an attempt to encounter a frog of the opposite sex, but, as we shall see later, sound also plays a role in numerous other situations: in the relationship between parents and their young, in the cohesion within family groups, in locating a prey or in escaping from a predator.

How can we listen to animal sound when we are also animals ourselves, with our own auditory capacities, our bodies, our life experience, our feelings? There are two distinct but compatible ways of listening to the sounds of nature: an aesthetic listening where sensations are of prime importance, and an analytical listening where questioning and knowledge take precedence. We can listen to a concerto or a symphony without understanding them and we can also study them, analyse them and discuss them according to the rules of musicology. The same is true when it comes to the sounds of nature: we can allow ourselves to be transported by the sound of a forest without understanding what we are hearing, and then we can analyse the sounds in detail in order to enhance our understanding.

Henry David Thoreau, the North American naturalist and philosopher, envies the unsophisticated way children hear sounds and admires their ability to love a sound purely for its own sake and for its intrinsic value.[3] We need to be sensitive to sound in its own right, unadorned, and without any artifice such as music or orchestration, like the creak of packed snow, the rustling of a white poplar or the sudden crackle of lightning. Most importantly we should love sound for sound's sake, whatever form it takes. We should love sound for its shape, its silhouette, its multiple dimensions, its depth, its delicacy, its power, its discretion, and come to accept its sometimes harsh and even abrasive quality. We should love the way sound takes unexpected directions, how it bounces back and beats out its rhythms. We should embrace its sudden changes of mood and its surprises. Enjoy its creaks, whistles, crackles and rattles, its ability to be melodic, rhythmic and reedy. We should embrace sound full-on, standing tall, our lungs full, on the summit of a mountain or in the bed of a river. We should be joyously attentive to the complete and all-encompassing sound emanating from an entire landscape and then seek out the details and the different elements. We should relish its sudden surges, its trills, vibrations, glissandi, its sharp spikes and muffled softness. We should listen to sound as a whole and then identify the individual sounds, stoop down to gather up little sounds from the forest floor and reach upwards to touch the sounds coming from the foliage overhead. Listening to sound in this manner means applying Pierre Schaeffer's principle of reduced listening, it means forgetting about the reasons behind the sound and concentrating instead on what is unique about it.

And we can also listen with a frown on our faces, we can turn our heads from side to side, cup our hands behind our ears, or resort to sophisticated and bulky equipment. We can listen in order to probe even deeper, to track down sound in a tree or amongst the ferns. We can be attentive, alert, not allowing ourselves to be carried away in a torrent of sound, refusing to believe that sound is uniform, setting off in quest of its variations in time, amplitude and frequency. We can listen so as to unravel and to gain a deeper understanding. We can develop an analytical approach to listening, breaking down what we hear into its various elements, in order to quench our curiosity, our thirst for knowledge. We can seek explanation through observation, experimentation and inference. We can revisit the laws of mathematics and of mechanics and call on the great names of sound: Hermann von Helmholtz, Jean Baptiste Joseph Fourier, David Hilbert, Harry Nyquist and Claude Shannon. We can turn to behavioural science and re-read Jean-Henri Fabre, Jakob von Uexküll, Nikolaas Tinbergen, Konrad Lorenz and Karl von Frisch. We can evoke the finest theories of evolutionary science with Charles Darwin's *natural selection* and *sexual selection*, Van Valen's *Red Queen*, John Krebs' *Beau Geste* or James Fisher's *Dear Enemy*. In order to broaden our listening experience, we can delve into the ecology of populations, of communities, of ecosystems or of landscapes in the company, amongst others, of Ernst Haeckel, George Hutchinson and Edward O. Wilson. We can also explore vibrating bodies acting as transmitters or receivers, seek help from biomechanics, from physiology, genetics or molecular biology. In so doing, we are choosing to listen in a scientific way, we are getting out our penknives and describing, analysing and experimenting as we continue to play like children in the depths of an unfenced garden.

Finally, and most importantly, we can combine the two ways of listening, indulging both our passion, by adopting the sensitive approach, and our curiosity, by favouring an analytical one. We can focus our attention on audiobiophilia, or in other words, the double appeal of sound and of nature. Audiophilia means a heightened attention to high-quality and unpolluted sounds, referred to as high-fidelity sounds. High-fidelity is essentially associated with listening to music using equipment capable of a very high quality of reproduction, but it could also be used to describe the act of listening to the sounds and silences of natural spaces which may themselves be of high quality.[4] Biophilia is 'the innate tendency to concentrate on life and on biological processes',[5] an indication therefore of a profound interest in natural history, and one which will be cultivated to varying extents throughout our lives, depending on our education and our personal experiences. *Audiobiophilia* therefore corresponds to an early and deep interest in the sounds of nature, an interest which deserves to be maintained throughout our lives through regular contact with living creatures, with their movements, their shapes, their colours and, of course, the world of sound they inhabit.

3

In the tropics

The warm, damp, rust-coloured earth of French Guiana exudes an ambiguous sensation of tropical exploration and European déjà vu. Here cultures, histories and people merge – Creoles, Noir Marron, Hmong, Amerindians, Brazilians – all gathered together under the aegis of a single French administration. From the moment you first arrive in Cayenne, your eye is caught by the tropical forest, vast and dense, but welcoming like a great-aunt with comforting curves. As the doors of the plane open, the tropical heat and humidity bring a sense of well-being, relaxing your muscles and making all tension melt away. On the busy road leading from the airport to the centre of Cayenne, a rain front moves in, already pounding on the metal roofs. This is a far cry from the fine, cold rain of Paris, for the air here is very different. We are in South America. We came expecting to find pulsating life, a buzz of street sellers and musicians, such as might be associated with Brazil or Colombia for example, but the streets of Cayenne, and of the other towns and villages, are surprisingly quiet outside the carnival season, when the whole place erupts in a party atmosphere. Arriving from Paris and for a completely unjustified reason, probably stemming from a desire to experience a sense of disorientation, you expect to arrive in a foreign country, but to your surprise, you find yourself in a familiar, recognizable landscape, with roads, roundabouts, traffic signs, shops, advertising hoardings and commercial centres identical in every respect to those found in any French suburb. We are in France. Guiana is a tropical corner of a Europeanized South America where traffic cameras control speed at the edges of forests in which sloths sleep and jaguars roar, where you can buy Vache qui Rit cheese and Normandy milk alongside mangos and ambarella juice.

Ever since my first visit in 2008, filled with trepidation at the idea of stepping into a forest I imagined full of danger and in which we were going to install a network of twenty or so microphones to record the murmuring sounds of the forest, I have managed to return on a number of occasions, each time with a growing feeling of attachment. Now, on grey suburban days, I dream of the colours of Guiana and its green treasure, this immense forest, crisscrossed with shady creeks and full of glossy plants and playful animals; in the summer, I stretch myself out, barefoot, in my Guyanese hammock and pretend that I am there.

Guiana is a favoured playground for French ecologists, ethnologists and other historians of nature. In 1986, following an initial venture set up by the Muséum national d'histoire naturelle, the Centre national de la recherche scientifique established a research station in the heart of the Nouragues Nature Reserve, one of the largest French nature reserves. Over the last thirty years, in this open-air laboratory, researchers have worked on the task of describing and understanding the structure and the workings of tropical biodiversity. Snakes, frogs, birds, insects, trees, mosses, parasites, bacteria and fungi are all closely observed with the aid of binoculars, microscopes or DNA sequencing.

So, on a number of occasions, I and various colleagues have found ourselves heading to Nouragues in order to get more closely acquainted with the forest. The research station is deliberately isolated and the nearest village is many kilometres away. To reach it from Cayenne you can either take a short ride in a helicopter – flown just above the forest canopy by a former French army officer, keen to tell you about his military exploits in former Yugoslavia – or you can make your way by land and water, first to Regina, a little village with a few hundred inhabitants but located in an area as vast as a *département* in metropolitan France, and then travel up the Approuague River in a dugout canoe.

On this occasion, in February 2019, we were making the journey of several hours on board a long wooden dugout piloted by Agaci, a Brazilian boatman with a charming smile. Our bags and suitcases, with their jumble of clothes and equipment reflecting our existence as researchers constantly mixing our private and professional lives, are stowed and protected in the bottom of the boat under large blue tarpaulins. This river trip is the start of a little adventure at the research station where four of us are going to study the propagation of sounds through the undergrowth and set up a permanent station for recording the sounds of the forest. Thanks to Agaci's deft handling of the dugout, the various waterfalls, which impose their sudden changes of mood on the riverbed and create small rapids, were easily negotiated and there was just a light rain blurring the sky and wetting our city-dwelling faces, thrilled to be leaving behind a European winter in exchange for tropical sunshine.

Travelling by river is a wonderful way of getting close to nature. All you need is to borrow a boat of some kind and let yourself be carried, mind and body, through the water and along the river banks. Water courses are open corridors where birds, migrating annually or just for a day, can be seen in broad daylight and the banks teem with animals in quest of water or sun. For those who know how to drift along the river without being heard, the entire spectrum of life on or near the water is theirs for the viewing.

The use of a powerful diesel engine does not permit this discretion. If Agaci can hear absolutely nothing of what is going on around him – neither the possible calls of passing birds, nor our impossibly convoluted discussions under the warm wind – he still manages to demonstrate his rich experience of the landscape. With a sudden unexpected gesture, he slows down, changes direction and heads straight for one of the tree-lined banks of the Arataye, a little tributary of the Approuague favoured by illegal gold prospectors, which we are now entering. He cuts the engine and we find ourselves enveloped in a languid, humid silence. A few metres away, on an old black tree trunk, a young grey caiman (*Paleosuchus trigona*) meditates indolently, warming his extraordinarily rough skin in the sun and basking in the newly rediscovered silence.

The noise of the engine soon resumes, for every minute counts on these rivers and it is preferable to arrive before night falls like a theatre curtain, unannounced and abrupt. After five hours of navigation, we arrive at the research station, a wonderful place occupied all year round by lucky academics and where the day-to-day running is in the hands of a diligent team of engineers and technicians. The camp consists of a cluster of huts linked by walkways and wooden staircases. The huts are spacious open constructions offering shelter from the rain and coloured hammocks in which to rock yourself to sleep. This camp is home only to experienced researchers who are conscientious and serious, working on well-constructed and thoroughly evaluated research projects and skilfully handling fragile and costly instruments. Nevertheless, observing them moving around in this environment brings to mind a troop of children with uncombed hair and grazed knees whose parents have constructed magical cabins for them, hidden at the bottom of a luxuriant garden. These researchers are not working – they are playing.

We unload our bags with the help of the residents and, before Agaci restarts his engine to set off for another site, we hunt through our things and present him with a set of the red noise-cancelling headphones which we plan to use for our experiments in propagating sounds. He thanks us with a broad smile the warmth of which stays with us for a long time. Protecting yourself from noise in order to enter a form of silence is surely no luxury.

The tropical forest is the apex of the earth's biodiversity. Here, climatic conditions have encouraged a greater number of plant and animal species than anywhere else. To give just one example, we decided to set up our recording station in a small isosceles triangle, its sides measuring 186 metres and demarcating a surface area of 1.5 hectares. In this little geometric area of forest, 172 species of trees grow, 213 species of birds fly, and twenty-six species of amphibians hop about. At different times of the day and night, of the seasons and the years, these birds and frogs add their songs and cries to the sounds of monkeys, bats, grasshoppers, locusts, crickets and cicadas. All of these multiple sounds produce an intense and unique acoustic atmosphere. This soundscape is not easy to describe; Chateaubriand found himself forced to abandon his attempts when trying to describe the alluvial forests of the Mississippi in the prologue to *Atala*: 'then such sounds came from the depths of the forests, such sights presented themselves to the eye, that I might try in vain to describe them to those who have never travelled the primitive fields of nature'.[1] Of course, the forest here is in no sense primitive and our scientific perspective is very far removed from Chateaubriand's more romantic viewpoint, but the difficulty remains the same, and is perhaps even more acute, given that, in the Amazon region, there is even greater diversity in terms of sound than there is on the banks of the Mississippi.

We should not however imagine a deafening acoustic chaos. The voice of the forest is rarely silent but quiet periods nevertheless occur, for example in the middle of the afternoon, when it seems to be drawing breath.

After several days familiarizing ourselves with the site, conducting tests and installing our equipment, the intensity of our field work eases off. I take advantage of the respite to spend some time on my own at dawn listening to, and recording, the forest waking up. Getting out of your hammock early, at five o'clock on this occasion, requires a certain effort. You need to be ready to get up in darkness, ensure your movements and the white halo of your headtorch do not disturb your colleagues still sleeping beneath their mosquito nets, pull on your boots, quietly gather up the material assembled the night before, pick up a security walkie-talkie and, at last, head into the forest alone. All that effort is rewarded a thousand times over: having the camp and then the forest to yourself is a privilege it would be a great pity to miss.

The path I take is a short one of just a few hundred metres, not much longer than the one I had taken in the Chartreuse mountains. I get my recording equipment ready, slightly fumbling with the buttons as always, and then stand completely still. It is still dark, and a few tardy insects and frogs continue to sing. I am finally alone with the sounds of the forest and that is exactly what I want. To get away in order to hear better. To hear, first of all, this deep, muffled sound I have already heard here in Guiana and also in Mexico, this acoustic force capable of penetrating the body and making it vibrate. This sound mass is well known to all those who have been fortunate enough to explore the forests of Central and South America, but still this chorus of voices broadcast to the entire forest never fails to impress. Howler monkeys shriek above the trees making everything around them vibrate. How and why do they make such a racket? The strength of their howls, one of the most powerful amongst terrestrial animals, comes from the vibration of a vocal sac lying in a ventral hyoid bone which has an unusual bowl-like shape. This laryngeal sac expands the throat, reducing frequencies and increasing the volume of the sound. Like the frog in La Fontaine's fable, the monkey is attempting to seem bigger than he is, probably in an extravagant attempt to mark his territory, avoid neighbouring groups or settle scores with his rivals. Whatever the reason, these shrieks make unforgettable sound memories. Nor are the monkeys alone. A host of different sounds comes from high and low. In a single minute of recording, it is possible to hear, alongside the monkeys, several species of frogs and birds and, above all, neglected and little known, a dozen different insects – probably crickets and grasshoppers – emitting sounds confined somewhere within a range of between 4 and 10 kilohertz. These little-known insects are the acoustic aura of the forest.

Day breaks, more gradually than the previous nightfall. I am on the point of going back to the camp with a number of recordings successfully completed when I suddenly become aware of a random rustling of leaves and the sound of snapping branches to my right. This is surprising in an environment where movements are generally rather stealthy. The noises continue and then, from the source of the disturbance, comes a series of sharp, intense barks which remind me of the sound of roe deer in the forest of Rambouillet. It is indeed two small deer, probably red brockets (*Mazama americana*). They are chasing each other around, leaping over the plants in the undergrowth. Their movements are unpredictable and I am unsure where to put myself, caught up in a kind of ballet where the choreography is unfamiliar to me. On the recording, I would hear my breath racing, and yet there was nothing to fear here – no jaguar, elephant, tiger, bear or monster. Just two elegant deer doing their pointe work on the humid forest floor.

Making my way back down to the huts, I realize that in that brief flurry of time I had been in a state of almost total calm. In this forest, noises are rare in the early morning: no supply helicopters, no distant canoes, no talkative researchers.

Far from humans, far from machines, deep in the acoustic merry-go-round of the tropical forest, I had once again, more than 7,000 kilometres away from the snowy Alps, stepped into another silence.

4

The nature of sounds

I was no more than a little pair of ears lost in some corner of a tropical forest. In the time it took for the sun to rise, I had unwittingly stepped into a paradox, another form of silence, a full-bodied, intense silence, rich in biological sounds and full of howls, shrieks, songs and the rustling of leaves. In this case, it was the absence of human sounds that had carved out a form of benevolent emptiness. This silence was a silence for nature, a silence for the naturalist, once again alone and motionless.

In a holistic vision, the *sonosphere*, like the concepts of biosphere and ecosphere which incorporate all the levels of organization of living systems, includes all terrestrial sounds, from across the whole planet, regardless of where they come from and how they are dissipated. This vast whole teems with sound, coming from left and right, from above and below, from in front and from behind, from the past, the present and yet to come. A trembling multitude which can be organized – and the naturalist has an innate talent for sorting, classifying and labelling – according to various different criteria such as, for example, the medium through which they are propagated (gas vs liquid vs solid), the nature of the sounds (biotic vs abiotic), their origin (animal vs plant vs mineral, human vs non-human), their function (as an indicator of the state of the environment, or of the status of another living creature, or as a way of establishing a social link), or else according to their physical properties (duration, amplitude, frequency and phase). Over the last few years, the sonosphere of natural landscapes, or soundscapes, has been classified into three distinct categories, depending on the nature of the sound source. These categories are *biophony*, which includes all biotic sounds originating from animals and plants; *geophony*, which corresponds to all naturally occurring but abiotic sounds; and *anthropophony*, which covers all sounds of human origin.[1]

There is little point in listing all the biophonic sounds since, in principle, any living being capable of movement, or in the process of moving, produces sound, since sound originates from a distortion of the immediate environment and therefore from a movement. Initially, the sound produced by the movement of all or part of a body is neither intentional nor controlled nor structured, but it exists, it occupies a place in the sonosphere, in the soundscape.

The common limpet (*Patella vulgata*) is a gastropod mollusc well known to children who enjoy exploring rock pools at low tide. Clinging tenaciously to the rock like an immovable Egyptian pyramid, the limpet appears immobile, a rock in its own right, impassively resisting squalls and breakers. This appearance is a deceptive one, for the limpet defends its territory in shellfish battles where it launches attacks on intruders, and sets off on forays covering distances of several tens of centimetres in order to graze elsewhere, though always returning to the same point of departure. Like a cow in its rich pasture, the limpet spends the hours between high tide and low tide grazing on the green seaweed which covers the dark rocks. The gastropod tears the seaweed off the rocks with repeated movements of the radula, a sort of rough tongue covered in denticles. Hard and resistant, the denticles scrape over the rock gathering the algal film and, in doing so, produce a rasping sound which, when considerable numbers of limpets are present on the same rock, is transformed into a continuous scraping sound.

The sound made by the limpet is completely incidental and does not appear to have any role in the biology of the mollusc or of other marine animals. Of course, the limpet is not alone in exhibiting a certain lack of manners by making a noise when eating. Almost all animals generate sound when eating or moving around – we need only think, for example, of the larvae of wood-feeding insects which bore through wood, of a leopard drinking at a water hole, of sheep chewing grass in the pasture, parrot-fish grazing on coral, a cricket landing on a dead leaf, a leaping dolphin, a bird beating its wings or a galloping horse. All movement is sound and fills the air with its vibrations. These sounds act as indicators of a change in the state of the surrounding environment, such as the arrival of other members of the same species, the proximity of an appetizing prey or, conversely, of an ill-intentioned predator. A single sound can trigger behaviour associated with flight, fight or the search for a partner. Because of its critical importance, a sound abruptly emerges from the background of other sounds, becoming clearer, like a head suddenly standing out above a group. This auditory salience can mark the beginning of acoustic communication and of the deliberate production of sounds.

Whatever their origin, the sounds of communication are the sounds of survival. They can stem from the same mechanism as incidental sounds but the physical movement involved becomes intentional and the production of sound is controlled and structured. The movement is declared, exposed, revealed to all. It is no longer an epiphenomenon but a deliberate act, an extension of the self, and that changes everything.

If intentional sounds do not appear to exist in plants – we are not yet aware of any plant species capable of deliberately producing sounds[2] – sound communication has, over the course of evolution, manifested itself independently on numerous occasions in different groups of animals including arthropods (insects, spiders, scorpions and crustaceans), fish, amphibians, reptiles, birds and mammals.

Evolution resulted in the development of a great many ways of producing sound. The simplest solution is where sound is associated with physical movement. Any form of movement can be enough to set up vibrations. Fruit flies and mosquitoes transform their wing beats into a love song, and pigeons use them as an alarm signal indicating flight from danger. Certain insects, like lacewings, those delicate green insects with lacy wings, tremble like leaves on the stems of plants. This quivering of the body, or tremulation, causes vibrations in plant tissue that are picked up by the feet of other members of the same species. In planthoppers, leafhoppers, treehoppers and other phytophagous cousins of the cicada, the physical movements come from folds in the trachea, the distortion of which produces vibrations. Sound can also be produced in a very intuitive way by simple percussion – the impact of the body against a solid object produces a sound at the interface of two media. Elephants stamp their feet for the benefit of members of the same species several kilometres away, humpback whales slap the sea with their pectoral or dorsal fins, chimpanzees drum on tree trunks, stoneflies tap their abdomens against stones on the river banks, jumping spiders beat the ground with their front legs, fiddler crabs strike the sand with their oversized claws, the woodworm or 'death watch beetles' that gnaw through our furniture bang their heads against the wood, and certain cicadas discreetly brush against branches with their diaphanous wings. More than 200,000 species of insects produce sounds through the vibration of another medium. A whole unsuspected world of sounds is beating time amongst our meadow plants.[3]

Using the body as a drum is also possible, though much rarer: certain Australian moths (*Hecatesia* spp.) play castanets with the reinforced edges of the veins in their wings, the Indian peafowl (*Pavo cristatus*) emits a very low sound by shaking its tail feathers, rattlesnakes (*Crotalus* spp.) shake and rattle the rings at the end of their tails, and the gorillas of the western lowlands (*Gorilla gorilla gorilla*) beat their chests and clap their hands in the depths of their African forests.

Stridulation is a mechanism similar to body percussion but rather than striking two body parts against each other, they are rubbed together, one acting as a fine-toothed comb and the other as a plectrum or scraper. This method requires hard parts which guarantee an impact when the plectrum strikes the comb and is therefore most common in arthropods with rigid chitinous outer bodies. Different parts of the body are used – the wings in crickets and grasshoppers, the legs in locusts, but also the heads of certain ground bugs, the thorax in beetles, the abdomen in ants, the tail in crayfish, the antennae in lobsters, the femur in spiders and the chelicerae in scorpions. Every part of the body can potentially become a source of stridulation and, here too, we should set aside any preconceptions and look for the most improbable possibilities, such as the millimetre-long penis of certain water boatmen (*Micronecta* spp.). Stridulation is much rarer in vertebrates. The club-winged manakin (*Machaeropterus deliciosus*), a bird native to the Colombian Andes, shows off to females by taking a bow, as etiquette demands, curving its wings above its body, and, in a shudder of ecstatic seduction, produces a harmonic sound of disarming beauty. The purity of the sound made by the feathers is due to the stridulation of some modified remiges, or wing feathers, which resonate together. Under the water, fish can also stridulate by grinding or rubbing together the bones of the skull, the gills, fins or certain vertebrae.

It is indeed amongst bony fish that another astonishing mechanism of sound production can be observed. Most species produce sound by squeezing and releasing their swim bladder with the help of specialized muscles which can contract rapidly. It is therefore by exerting pressure on this gas-filled pocket that fish bellow softly underwater, producing pulsating, low and sepulchral sounds.

Several insects make themselves heard by distorting one part of their rigid bodies, often in the form of a rod-like structure made of chitin and resilin, molecules which ensure resistance and elasticity. So, for example, the blue-winged grasshopper (*Oedipoda caerulescens*), a very common grasshopper, produces a crackling sound as it makes its escape from under our enormous feet, revealing its turquoise wings as it does so. In the case of the peacock butterfly (*Inachis io*), a European butterfly with blue eye-spots, picked out with red, and probably also that of the blue cracker or variable cracker (*Hamadryas feronia*), a South American butterfly with marbled wings, the veins on the wings distort and produce a clicking sound, ultrasonic in peacocks, and potentially audible in the case of the blue cracker. The mechanism involved is somewhat similar to the click made by squeezing a hair slide: one *click* as it is opened and another *click* when it closes. A similar principle exists in somewhat more complex anatomical constructions exclusively dedicated to the production of sound. Certain moths have a pair of cymbals hidden in their abdomen. These consist of a stretched membrane, sometimes with a grooved surface, held within a rigid frame. Strong dorsal muscles distort the frame and the membrane, producing ultrasonic clicking noises during mating or in the never-ending combat with bats. In cicadas, the cymbals are unique organs, usually visible on the side of the first segments of the abdomen. These cymbals are membranes in the shape of a rugby ball, supported by a series of long and short rods. Two enlarged muscles pull against these, causing a clicking sound each time the rod is distorted. The resulting stream of clicks produced by the cicada are like the sounds emerging from a railway tunnel running through the white mountains of Provence, thus giving rise to the 'coppery hum' so dear to Marcel Pagnol.[4]

Pistol shrimps (*Alpheus* spp. and other species of the Alpheidae family) owe their name to one of their pincers, which is disproportionately large, measuring up to half their body length, and which produces an extremely loud snapping sound when it closes. The repetition of these explosions coming from thousands of individuals creates an underwater crackling sound which can be detected almost anywhere in the world simply by putting your head underwater near submerged rocks. This pincer consists of two moveable and interlocking parts, a piston and a cavity. The closing of the pincer is so powerful and so fast – something in the order of 100 kilometres per hour – that the water present in the cavity is expelled by the action of the piston. A cavitation bubble then forms, in other words a phenomenon of intensely low pressure. This is the result of the implosion – and not the explosion – of the bubble, which produces the acoustic vibration so characteristic of the ocean floor.

Finally, there are what are generally regarded as the more classic methods of sound production, given that these are the ones used by humans, namely those which correspond to the passage of air through a tube or orifice with sometimes resonant properties. Whistling, for example, consists in simply expelling air under pressure and causing a cavity to vibrate. Very few insects use this technique, but the males of certain cockroaches from Madagascar (*Gromphadorhina* spp., *Elliptorhina* spp.) whistle gallantly for the benefit of any females in the vicinity. The tracheae of the first abdominal segment appear to be modified and are wider and longer than the others, opening to the exterior through a valve, a spiracle, which is much bigger. The compression of the trachea forces the air contained inside it to be expelled through the spiracle producing delicate whistling or hissing sounds. The caterpillars of the walnut sphinx moth (*Amorpha juglandis*) behave in a similar manner when under attack. The hissing of snakes, which is generally largely unstructured and without any real temporal or frequential organization, results from a simple hyperventilation since their small larynx plays no role in the production of sound. Dolphins, which also have a reduced larynx, whistle like mermaids, producing quick, complex, shrill sounds, not easily detected by our ears, adapted as they are to our slow, deep utterances.

The capacity to produce sound takes a different form when the larynx, equipped with vocal cords, becomes involved. When this is the case, both reptiles – but particularly frogs, as in the case of the green tree frog – and mammals manage to produce a very wide spectrum of sounds. They may be shrill or deep, fast or slow, and can be continuous or modulated in frequency and amplitude, allowing a variety of information to be shared in a great many behavioural contexts, ranging from distress to the subtleties of communication between parents and their young. Air causes the vocal cords to vibrate and these vibrations travel into the oral cavity, in particular to the pharynx, amplifying certain frequencies and therefore producing a tone which can sometimes be unique. The same is more or less true for birds, though instead of a pharynx these have a syrinx situated much further down the respiratory organs, just above the point where the two bronchial tubes diverge. This syrinx is remarkable in that it is double, being made up of two pairs of vibrating membranes at the opening of each of the bronchial tubes. This doubling of the vocal organ allows the bird to sing with one or two voices alternately or simultaneously, opening up unique possibilities for acoustic invention and composition.

Animals use their wings, their feet, their abdomens and their throats to produce sound. All these different anatomical ways of projecting a sound into the environment are not necessarily sufficient, since the acoustic battle between members of the same species or between two different species often means that sound energy needs to be concentrated onto certain frequencies and the sound has to be projected over as great a distance as possible. Singing loudly is therefore a way of warding off enemies and attracting friends over the greatest possible distance. In order for that to happen, it is sometimes necessary to turn to external objects, which are used less as tools than as accessories shaped in such a way as to allow them to filter and amplify the sound as it emerges from the body. Many different solutions have been found – crickets use leaves from trees as diffusers to improve their acoustic range, mole crickets dig tunnels which act as acoustic cones, frogs sit inside hollow and echoing tree trunks, fish murmur inside pearl oysters using the shell as an amplifier, bats hide in tube-shaped leaves which have all the properties of an acoustic horn. Animals find extensions of themselves in the objects, bodies and living creatures that surround them and these help them in their efforts to communicate with others. True engineers, they know where to position themselves in the environment, just as the studio musician marks his position on the floor with a cross made of sticky tape. In the case of cicadas, frogs and birds, the choice regarding the height of their singing post seems, amongst other elements, to minimize the possibility that their songs will be impeded by the surrounding vegetation and reduces the risks of interference from other sound-producing species. Even if this is still poorly documented, it seems likely that animals also choose a singing post which corresponds to a strategic location depending on the scale of a particular landscape: a high and dominant vantage point, somewhere unencumbered by obstacles, or any other place which offers advantages in terms of acoustics. We might therefore suppose that wolves, elephants, monkeys or whales select sites which maximize the range of their sound proclamations.

The immediate environment is both friend and enemy to the singer. A friend because it alone is capable of transmitting the message by vibrating along with the singer, and an enemy because it obstructs the propagation of the signal with the obstacles which are an intrinsic part of it – trees, seaweed, rocks or walls – and can therefore sabotage any hope of reaching a well-disposed ear. Sound spreads in all kinds of environment, from the Arctic icefields to the Antarctic Plateau and including forests, savannahs, prairies, fields, deserts, hills, mountains, skies, rivers, ponds, seas, oceans and even human constructions. There are few places where animal sound does not exist.

Wherever they live, wherever they roam, in whatever way they produce sound, animals unwittingly leave clues or deliberately exchange information. In all cases, they give meaning to the sounds they produce, using them to draw attention to the states and behaviours which matter in their lives.

First of all, there are all the indicators and signals which govern hostile interactions between prey and predator. The two protagonists can leave sound traces in the surrounding environment which enable them to detect each other and therefore trigger a fight or flight reaction. When the predator is detected, the prey can resort to different sound expressions. The first is a defence signal where the desired outcome is the retreat of the predator, as in the case of many reptiles which, when confronted with a bigger or more dangerous animal, puff themselves up, blow, hiss and therefore give warning of a probable attack. The second possible reaction is one of altruistic alarm – a warning sent to their family or to other members of the species in the form of a sound which indicates the presence of danger. So, for example, monkeys, birds, squirrels and meerkats sound the alarm and trigger reactions of flight or of defence amongst other members of the group. The third reaction is one of last resort. It involves a sound of distress made by the prey when it is seized upon by the predator, a final attempt to force it to release its grip or a desperate call for help addressed to the family group or members of the same species. Distress signals are very common amongst animals ranging from bats to crocodiles and including dung beetles. They may represent one of the first sound expressions to appear in the course of evolution, a reflex reaction in response to a situation of maximum stress.

Landscapes emit sounds which can be used for animal orientation. This ability to pick up sound clues in order to navigate through the immediate environment is poorly understood, but recent observations show that certain fish larvae and marine mussels use the sounds of their environment as sound markers, that pigeons can find their way thanks to an infrasonic map during their long homing journeys and, finally, that certain species, in particular amphibians, use the sounds made by others in order to locate each other.

Orientation in space is also used much more actively by bats, toothed whales and some rare birds, which emit signals into the surrounding environment and analyse the echoes these produce. These biosonar signals, often ultrasonic in order to obtain a high spatial resolution, provide a detailed image of the surrounding environment including its topography, textures and the whereabouts of any moving objects. Sounds and their distorting mirrors supply information vital to moving around. Whether on their own or combined with smells, tastes, colours, movements, touch and electrical discharges, sounds play a role in reproductive behaviour. Signals marking a sexual territory, call signals over a long distance, mating calls from near at hand, signals of rivalry between two eager rivals or signals indicating the rejection of an over-insistent suitor all have a role to play in encounters with sexual partners. The form these take are the result of sexual selection, that is to say of the evolutionary forces involved in competition between individuals of the same sex – often males – in quest of favours from the other sex, capable of exerting choice – often females. These signals contain coded information on species, gender and individual qualities, all essential for effective reproduction with a strong chance of survival. There are countless examples of this but the roar of a rutting stag which vibrates through the branches each autumn is a fine demonstration of what sexual selection can produce – a deep, intense, full-bodied, overwhelming and irresistible roar which drives away brazen young rivals and draws females.

Finally, sound signals are a way of ensuring a bond, social cohesion in a broad sense, wherever there is an obvious advantage in remaining together. That is why we hear contact calls between individuals moving as a group, like birds migrating across continents and seas, or elephants who synchronize their movements, without necessarily being able to see each other, thanks to infrasounds, or between parents and young seals who recognize each other by their calls. In this way, couples, families and groups are linked together by vibrating threads.

This diversity in terms of species, methods and approaches gives rise to an astonishing acoustic diversity. Variations are seemingly endless whether in terms of modulations, tempi, rhythms, nuances or tone. The possibilities seem endless, whether solo, as a duo or in chorus. We need to learn to stop, close our eyes and savour this multiplicity of sounds made up of clicks and of sonic glissandos, slow or fast, whispered or bellowed, until, suddenly, we come to the realization that, even in the middle of a built-up urban area, between the glass towers and above the concrete pavements, the song of a bird contains as many sounds as there are flowers in an alpine meadow. Audiobiophilia is rare because, in our interiorized way of living, there is little need for it. We no longer listen to birds. Why have we distanced ourselves so much from biophony? Probably because it is no longer regarded as useful since more than 80 per cent of us are now city-dwellers and the sounds of nature do not bring us the information we need for the smooth running of our modern lives. What is the point of knowing that a mistle thrush is singing at the edge of our open spaces? What difference does it make to our lives to recognize the croaking sounds of the frog that lives in the neighbour's pond? And what are we to make of the sounds made by a fly knocking against the window? The only sounds we still pay some attention to are those which might herald a minor danger, like the whirring wings of an Asian hornet, the scuffling of a mouse which has had the temerity to come in without knocking, or the swish of a bird flying too close to our heads. There is also still some vestigial interest in the sounds of geophony, which can provide us with information about a meteorological state or help us find our way over great distances.

Geophony groups together sounds coming from Empedocles's four elements of earth, water, fire and wind. The writings of John Muir, a pioneer of ecology in the nineteenth century who grew up in the predominantly mineral environment of the high mountains of North America, demonstrate the importance of these sounds in the construction of natural landscapes: the scraping and crashing of falling stones, the songs and melodies of running water, the whistling and rustling of the wind in the sequoias and giant redwoods.[5]

The sounds of the earth are probably those most deeply rooted in the history of life even if we are not aware of all of them. This is the case, for example, with telluric vibrations, which can only be detected with the aid of seismometers. The earth is shaken continuously by weak but regular waves. First of all, free oscillations are observed every two to eight minutes, probably linked to ocean movements of very low frequencies. In addition to these oscillations, a steady throbbing is recorded every twenty-six seconds and this travels through the earth at a speed of more than 3 kilometres per second. The geographical origin of this other telluric sound has been localized in the Gulf of Guinea, near the island of São Tomé, and its mechanical origin appears to come from the impact of Atlantic Ocean waves breaking on the earth's crust. Finally, the earth is traversed with micro-earthquakes which are also linked to the oceans, though in this case, to the constant, regular swell of waves as the result of storms with frequencies of the order of several dozen millihertz. In this way, ocean movements, whether slow and on a global scale or rapid and local, generate a sequence of seismic waves which cause our planet to vibrate constantly, making it an intrinsic source of sound.

Earthquakes, both on the land and under the sea, generate waves which are clearly perceptible to everyone. Many observations report stress or flight behaviour in fish, amphibians, reptiles, birds and mammals prior to catastrophes – in other words, before walls start shaking or waves come crashing onto beaches. Such animals appear to be capable of picking up geophysical warning signs in the form of the waves known as primary waves (P), which travel longitudinally and more rapidly than secondary waves (S) with their more destructive shearing movement.

Less dramatic, the aquatic elements of natural landscapes produce sounds which are perfectly audible to the majority of animals: the crash of the surf, the eddies of a river or stream, the roar of a waterfall, the sound of melting snow, the movement of a glacier, the splitting of an iceberg. Thanks to its movements or changes of state, water vibrates and causes objects around it to vibrate. All these sounds make up the acoustic signature of landscapes and can act as sound markers during a journey or when seeking a water source.

Meteorological phenomena also generate a range of sounds. Snow falling softly from the sky or from trees in the great melt creates soft sounds and the snow cover exerts an influence on a soundscape, absorbing other sounds. Rain, sometimes falling torrentially during a violent storm, is an important feature of soundscapes, especially in tropical forests where the beating of water on vegetation produces such a din that it becomes impossible to speak. The sound of rain drumming on the ground produces a recognized effect on certain animals, notably bringing earthworms to the surface and causing frogs buried in the sand to emerge. Bats (*Micronycteris microtis*, *Molossus molossus*) wait for the sound of the rain to stop before coming out of their shelters to hunt, and the tawny owl (*Strix aluco*) is disturbed by the sound of rain, calling less on rainy nights than on dry ones.

Wind is another sound element of natural environments. Unless it encounters obstacles, wind has no acoustic impact. Its presence is indicated by plant masses and animals. Trunks, stems, branches and leaves bend, move and vibrate in the wind and their movements are transformed into sound. They become the instruments and musicians of the wind. Bodies – ours, theirs – create air movements and vortexes which then become sounds. Wind also interferes with the communication of sound. So, for example, when adult king penguins (*Aptenodytes patagonicus*) return to land after a period of time in the sea, they have to repeat their display cry more often in order to be reunited with their mate when the wind is blowing over the ice floes.[6]

Amongst all the sound examples mentioned so far, whether related to biophony or geophony, human sounds appear to have been forgotten. This exclusion of man from other living creatures should not be seen as a manifestation of some form of speciesism. Indeed, naturalists are the first to emphasize that the human is just as much an animal as others. Nevertheless, man is a hegemonic being who constantly seeks to demonstrate his power, not over nature but against nature, by resorting to the use of loud sounds. Raised voices, booming music and noisy machinery invade the acoustic world of animals, drowning out the sounds of other animals. Human acoustic activity occupies a major space in the sonosphere and exerts a powerful influence on soundscapes, often with disruptive, even polluting effects. It is therefore reasonably logical to allocate it a separate place of its own – the realm of anthropophony.

5

In the heart of the Jura

There are too many of us. Too many to listen to the gentle breath of the forest deep in its winter dormancy. We talk too much and our excited voices drown out the subtle sounds of the coldest forest in France. And yet we are happy to be here and to be together, sharing our feelings, our experiences and our eagerness to work with, and for, this mysterious forest. It is February 2018, and we are walking with our new companions from the Parc Naturel Régional du Haut-Jura who are guiding us on our first trip across the peaceful white landscape of the Risoux forest.

The Risoux is a vast forest area situated on the eastern edges of France, along the border with Switzerland. Forests do not recognize borders and the French Risoux passes unchallenged across the old drystone boundary wall and continues as the Swiss Risoud forest. It is strange to cross this frontier so easily and fearlessly, in full daylight and without a care in the world, our ears listening attentively to the busy chatter of birds, whereas, during the Second World War, men, women and children crossed it by night, in the cold and in total darkness, deeply afraid of its terrible occupier and clinging desperately to the fragile hope of a free life.

The first stage of our exploration of the Risoux takes place in the depths of winter. Snow softens the contours of the mountains and the Jura landscape is crisply outlined against the deep blue January sky. Our companions urge us to come back in the summer, when everything is so different, when, over there, is a mass of bilberries, and there, meadows dotted with yellow gentian, and here, where we are standing, the ground is a metre lower once the snow has melted. Of course, we did come back in the summer and in the autumn, though less often in the spring – for fear of disturbing 'the Bird'.

The heart of the forest, wedged in a windy anticline, is spruce forest (*Picea abies*) mixed around the edges with beech trees (*Fagus sylvatica*), silver firs (*Abies alba*) and sycamores (*Acer pseudoplatanus*). The trees are rooted in a karstic soil where acid rainfall forms holes and deep cracks everywhere, treacherously concealed under a soft carpet of moss and bilberries. You can lose everything here – a pen, a microphone, a pair of binoculars, an ankle, or a friend. And it is here, on this crumbling ground and between century-old spruce trees, small and solid like grasshopper femurs, that 'the Bird' occasionally makes its appearance.

Straddling the municipalities of Morez, Bois d'Amont and Les Rousses, the Risoux forest is an extraordinary site because of its climate, fauna and flora. As a result, it qualifies for numerous protection measures (zone Natura 2000, natural area of interest for flora and fauna, prefectorial decree for protection of the biotope, regional natural park), although none of these seem to stop hunting or forestry activities both of which, according to a fine political euphemism, are beneficial for controlling animal populations and for thinning out the forest cover. The ancient forest is home to a great number of remarkable birds: the black woodpecker (*Dryocopus martius*) and the Eurasian three-toed woodpecker (*Picoides tridactylus*); the Eurasian pygmy owl (*Glaucidium passerinum*) and the boreal owl (*Aegolius funereus*) – the former hollowing out homes for the latter with their sharp beaks; the hazel grouse (*Tetrastes bonasia*) and the Eurasian woodcock (*Scolopax rusticola*); as well as the wolf (*Canis lupus*) and the Eurasian lynx (*Lynx lynx*). But the king of the Jura jungle, the quetzal of the Risoux, is none of those. The king is a cock, the queen is a hen. 'The Bird' in question is the western capercaillie (*Tetrao urogallus*), resplendent in its black, brown and metallic green plumage and its red eye-makeup.

The Risoux is an exceptional landscape. And yet, when we walk through the snow to familiarize ourselves with this landscape or to search for 'the Bird', we very often find ourselves looking skywards, not in order to identify a passing insect but to follow the trail of an aeroplane flying over Europe and carrying tourists to Ibiza, Porto, Barcelona or Marrakech. Each time, there is the low sound of engines adjusting their speed, this noise that seems to descend on us like bad news, this black cloud which sullies the landscape and fills our ears whether we like it or not, this physiological and psychological assault which is repeated every five minutes. Another plane, and then another one. And we are all too acutely aware that these passing planes are destroying both the soil and the trees of the Risoux, just like a pot of paint spilled onto a masterpiece. Up there, the airline companies, the pilots, the tourists, sometimes including ourselves, are in the process of contaminating an entire forest without realizing it and are passing by without even a gesture of apology.

6

The enemy

Noise, the enemy of silence, makes no attempt to disguise itself. It is an insidious and large-scale enemy which makes itself heard at all times and in all circumstances, often proud of its power. Omnipresent, it is coarse matter where silence is ethereal antimatter.

Sound, in its physical acceptance, is a longitudinal mechanical wave made up of variations in amplitude, duration, frequency and phase. The croaking of the green tree frog represents a physical structure in that its properties seem to be organized so as to form a coherent and predictable whole. Anyone who listens to this croaking for a few minutes, or even a few seconds, can grasp its form and momentum and, since the frog repeats a great deal, can also predict with reasonable confidence what the tree frog will sing a few minutes later. Noise is the exact opposite since it is effectively a sound with properties which do not have any specific organization but instead a random, even chaotic, profile. Amplitude, like the other physical properties, can climb, fall, stagnate or disappear without warning.

Animal sound production systems can sometimes contain a noisy element, a chaotic interval where glissandi or harmonics are replaced by noise. This occurs in numerous species which push their vocal equipment beyond the normal laws of physics, veering from an organized and modellable system towards something uncontrollable and unpredictable. The voices of rhesus monkeys (*Macaca mulatta*), zebra finches (*Taeniopygia guttata*), concave-eared torrent frogs (*Odorrana tormotus*), Australian freshwater lion fish (*Batrochomoeus trispinosus*) or dwarf hissing cockroaches (*Elliptorphina chopardi*) can go off track in this manner.

Noise therefore is not necessarily what we might think but is capable of insinuating its way into vocal productions which are ostensibly sweet and fluting. In reality, the notion of noise lies not just in the form taken by the sound but also in its content or, in other words, the meaning it brings to the receiver. As we know already, the male tree frog squatting at the edge of the pond announces his location, his specific identity, his gender, his availability and his individual qualities. In doing so, he sends out a certain amount of information which is decoded and interpreted by the other tree frogs in the area, who then react by croaking themselves (jealous males) or by approaching with what seems like a show of interest (timid females). The theory of information, as defined by Claude Shannon and Warren Weaver shortly after the Second World War, proposes a very simple framework to illustrate the rules governing the exchange of functional information as in the case of the tree frog.[1] On one side is a sound source, a transmitter – in this case the male tree frog – which sends out a signal containing information hidden in the form of a code based on variations of amplitude, duration, frequency and phase. Then, around this transmitter there is a transmission channel which carries the signal to a receiver capable of detecting it and decoding the hidden information it contains. From this information, the receiver draws their conclusions and reacts accordingly, with a physiological or behavioural response such as a croaking sound or a movement.

This principle may appear very simple – and in reality, it is – but it provides the model for a great many animal sound communication systems and enables another definition of noise to be introduced. The model of transmitter-channel-receiver-response is highly functional as long as the effects of external disturbance are not taken into account. However, still according to Shannon and Weaver, transmission in the channel between the transmitter and the receiver can be disrupted by the presence of other sounds which, whether emitted by chance or deliberately, can end up reducing, or even destroying, the information carried by the sound. Noise can be defined as all these disruptive external sounds.

The information sent by the green tree frog can be impaired by many different types of noise: the drumming of rain falling on the water lily leaves, the screeching of car tyres on the road, the roar of aeroplane engines overhead, but also, perhaps, the call of a passing bird, the sounds produced by the males of another species such as the marsh frog (*Pelophylax ridibundus*), or even by a male of its own species.

Noise is therefore not necessarily loud and chaotic but can be soft and structured, even musical at times. Noise is a sound which gets in the way, regardless of what form it takes. What is perceived as noise by some often turns out to be a signal for others. Think of a discussion you are trying to have in a crowded café. All the conversations around you are made up of signals packed with information exchanged by other people. Their signals are your noise and the signals you are attempting to share with your interlocutor represent noise for other people. The chatter of socialites at a cocktail party bears a certain resemblance to that of frogs in a puddle of water.

Noise therefore is a sound which is undesirable and unwelcome. It is astonishing to see how often the terms *sound* and *noise* are confused. We speak about bird noise or natural noises but is the blackbird's song at dawn really a nuisance? In principle, no, even if there are those who would prefer the cicadas to stop their chirping[2] during siesta time or who wish overexcited frogs could be a bit quieter come bedtime. The confusion between noise and sound is common in our conversations, in the media and in the arts, for example in scientific publications such as *The Soundscape* by Canadian academic and musician Raymond Murray Schafer, in which all sounds are noises. In the context of literature, Vladimir Nabokov, writer and naturalist, wrote a story in 1923 entitled Звуки in Russian, which would be translated as *Sounds* in English but as *Bruits* (noises) in French, even though none of the sounds encountered by the characters are in any way distressing. On the contrary, they are the signs of hidden but happy love stories, as is evident in this subtle juxtaposition of rain falling on the window and a Bach fugue, played by the woman who is the target of the narrator's admiration: 'I had a feeling of enraptured equilibrium as I sensed the musical relationship between the silvery specters of rain and your inclined shoulders, which would give a shudder when you pressed your fingers into the rippling luster.'[3]

As soon as sound gets in the way it becomes noise. For the non-domestic animal, in other words, the animal which derives no advantage from sharing its space with humans, all the sounds of anthropophony are in principle noises: the hum of cars, the rumbling of lorries, the roar of motorbikes, the throb of scooters, the drone of quadbikes, the whistling of trains, the grumble of planes, the whir of helicopters, the pointless growl of jet-skis, the whine of outboard motors, the chug of barges, the two-time beat of dugout canoes, the screech of brakes, the hooting of horns, the constant bleeping of parking censors, the reverberation of telephones ringing, the beep of notifications, the tinkling of bicycle bells, the jingling of doorbells, the thump of hammers, the crash of axes, the throb of drills, the hiss of blow-torches, the pounding of offshore oil rigs, the crack of weapons, the terrifying muffled boom of falling bombs, the blaring of military radars, the rasp of circular saws, the patter of garden sprinkler systems, the scratching of sanders, the jagged whir of chainsaws, the buzz of hedge-trimmers, the growl of mowers, the screech of stump cutters, the squeal of glass-blowers, the ruckus of mulchers, the hum of hoovers, the swoosh of electric fans, the throb of wind turbines, the crackling of high-voltage lines, the relentless murmur of generators, the clicking of irrigation pumps, the purring of air-conditioning units, the chatter of voices, the clamour of demonstrators, the steady rhythm of chants, the hubbub of music, the swish of a group of runners, the clacking of high heels, the nocturnal drone of factories, the wailing of sirens, the ticking of watches, the swinging of pendulums, the braying of hunting horns, the metallic tap of pétanque balls, the sigh of cables, the crackle of fireworks, the whistles of policemen and stationmasters and even the rustle of a flimsy dress.

A whole tidal wave of noises threatening to engulf animals to saturation point.

It is perhaps somewhat Manichean to see only noise and commotion in the sounds produced by humans with, on the one hand, a non-human nature seen as an innocent victim and, on the other, a distorted humanity imposing the power of its sounds. It is undoubtedly preferable to see man as an animal species evolving alongside other species. Human and non-human sounds should be capable of existing harmoniously without ever becoming noises to the other side. Nevertheless, the human sound print is ubiquitous and continuous.

Man does not like noise but likes to make noise. For those who are lucky enough to be able to hear, there is reassurance to be had from making noise. Since sound is movement and movement is life, making noise is one of the proofs which demonstrate that we are alive. What would happen if our movements were to become totally silent? How could we walk without hearing the swaying motion of our arms and the rhythm of our footsteps? How could we run our fingers through our hair without an accompanying swishing sound?

How could we breathe without hearing the air moving in and out of our nostrils? We would become transparent and our silent hands would pass through our heads and our bodies. We need an acoustic response, an echo telling us: 'You exist.' Making sound is an essential part of being alive. Yet we need to exercise some measure of subtlety and make sure we are not more alive than others.

Making noise is exhilarating. Who has not experienced a certain sense of power on a moped, a motorbike, in a car or a boat travelling at speed and defying the passing of time? Noise is the expression of an individual strength which we imagine renders us attractive. Noise allows us to be more widely visible, to impose ourselves on others, often with the help of machines we scarcely know how to use, but where simply applying a little pressure with a foot on a pedal or twisting our wrist on a handlebar produces dramatic effects. We are transformed from being small and puny to being tall and strong, handsome and powerful and ready to seduce. Noise is undoubtedly the expression of a secondary sexual characteristic, in other words, a marker of our gender which is transformed into an accessory designed to enhance seduction. In animals, particularly males, secondary sexual characteristics take the form of coloured markings, of enlarged or distorted body parts. Through a knock-on effect, sexual selection sometimes results in extravagant seduction tools such as a deer's antlers, a peacock's tail, the dumbbell-shaped eyes of the stalk-eyed fly, the treehopper's extraordinary thorax, or the giant mandibles of certain beetles. The same applies to those sound signals which, as a result of competition between the seducing males, are selected from one generation to the next for their low frequencies and their power. The deeper and louder the sound, the more securely the code containing any critical data is preserved. This principle leads certain species to a form of exaggeration where they produce sounds that are deeper than the size of their bodies would normally allow, thanks to anatomical contrivances such as the enlarged abdomens of certain cicadas, or the vocal sacs of frogs or of American howler monkeys which proclaim their presence to an entire forest.[4] The bikers we all of us are, to some extent or another, certainly behave in this way, using mechanical and acoustic devices in order to pretend that we are stronger and hoping to attract favourable attention from others. This seduction technique draws us into the noise trap, peppering our towns and our countryside with our intolerable racket.

The burden imposed by anthropophony is relentless. Our machines for extracting energy, our construction and destruction, our creations and transformations of matter, our constant movement, our leisure activities and our wars are happening everywhere. This technophony invades the ground with mineworkings and drilling for oil and gas but also exists on a daily basis with transport systems, work and leisure.[5] As a result, the earth is traversed with constant sounds, with seismic waves exclusively produced by humans and capable of disrupting animal and plant life. All aquatic environments – lakes, pools, ponds, torrents, streams, rivers great and small – are also rendered noisy by man, who diverts watercourses, installs dams, turbines, motors and hydraulic pumps or who travels in boats and motorized submarines. Insects, crustaceans and fish live therefore in environments where human noise is a constant presence.[6] Under oceans and seas, the presence of sonars, civil and military boats and vessels prospecting for fossil fuel has led to a doubling of noise levels every ten years.[7] Marine soundscapes are undergoing drastic change with a reduction in biological sounds and an increase in anthropic noises which have detrimental effects on invertebrates, fish, mammals and marine birds.[8] By the same token, human sounds are omnipresent on the earth and in the air, across all environments and all regions.

But in what way exactly do all these sounds constitute noise? Why not simply consider them as elements of a whole, as legitimate constituents of the sonosphere alongside the howling of wolves and the singing of whales? Primarily this is not possible because the majority of these sounds lack structure and do not have temporal or frequential definition, thereby corresponding to the physical definition of noise. Moreover, human sounds, in most cases, have negative impacts on behaviour, physiology and ecology. From the animal point of view, human sound satisfies the second definition of noise. Anthropophony is therefore unquestionably noisy for non-human living creatures.

The consequences of human noises on living beings are multiple, overlapping and inevitable.[9] Above all, human sounds affect those animals which communicate via sound or use sound as a tool to help them survive. Human noises superimpose themselves over the croaking of the green tree frog and the sounds produced by other amphibians, reptiles, arthropods, fish, birds and mammals. They interfere with messages by destroying the modulations of amplitude, time and frequency, by disrupting the spacing of phases. The code becomes unintelligible and the transfer of information impossible. Disrupting communication potentially means destroying a survival bond between parents and hungry offspring, it means preventing reproduction and damaging family and social bonds. Being unable to pick up sound clues in the surrounding area increases the risk of being caught by a predator, of failing to find sufficient food, or of taking the wrong direction and getting irretrievably lost.

The negative effects of human noises are not however limited to sound-producing species but can also affect species which hear even if they do not sing, species which do not have auditory organs but which nevertheless pick up sounds through their bodies, like molluscs for example.[10]

Sound, emitted at full power, can be a weapon, destroying the tympanic membranes or causing other damage to the middle ear. The US military are all too familiar with this and have already developed ultrapowerful weapons for use against pirates or to force demonstrators to retreat. In animals, intense noise can cause temporary or definitive damage to hearing in marine mammals after no more than just a few minutes exposure. They can suffer distortion of the tympan, destruction of cochlear hair cells, changes in cochlear blood pressure or the swelling of nerve cells due to glutamate poisoning. In response to the sound radars of boats and submarines, dolphins and toothed whales demonstrate signs of loss of sensitivity, and therefore forms of hearing loss.

Less traumatic, but in the end probably just as serious, noise has a disruptive effect on the body, causing a drop in concentration, lower attention levels, a reduction in learning capacity and sleep disturbances. Noise therefore generates stress which manifests itself in the form of behavioural disorders, endocrine disruption, cardiovascular problems and immune imbalances. Returning to the case of the green tree frog, traffic noise raises levels of stress hormones, resulting in immunosuppression and de-coloration of the vocal sac. All these physiological and morphological changes have behavioural consequences affecting both sound and visual communication in the frogs when they need to select their sexual partners.[11] The genetic effects amongst the population can be significant and can affect the viability of populations living along the roadside.

The repercussions of noise rarely occur in isolation. Instead, they overlap and interconnect and end up having a knock-on effect, like dominos collapsing on top of each other. As well as the direct mechanical and physiological effects there are also ecological consequences which go beyond an individual scale. Individuals do not live in a bubble but interact, positively or negatively, with their environment. They are consumers, prey, predators, builders, seed spreaders, pollinators, cleaners, regulators or even farmers. If their bodies and their biology are impaired as a result of noise, their ecological functions are also affected and, gradually, the consequences spread within ecological networks. The operation of oil wells in New Mexico generates high-density noise of around 95 decibels measured at 1 metre, equivalent in intensity to the noise of a motorway. These wells are installed in natural environments of woodland made up of junipers (*Juniperus osteosperma*) and pine (*Pinus edulis*), the seeds of which are eaten or dispersed by a series of mammals such as mice (*Peromyscus* spp.) and birds like the Californian scrub jay (*Aphelocoma californica*). The wooded landscape is dotted with a common North American flower (*Ipomopsis aggregata*), a member of the phlox family. This flower with its long, scarlet, tubulated corolla is pollinated by the black-chinned hummingbird (*Archilochus alexandri*). As the oil wells do not all operate at the same time, it is possible to compare noise-free sites with noisy sites. Astonishingly, pollination by the black-chinned hummingbirds is more successful in the noisy sites because the hummingbird's predators are less present as a result of the noise – their absence makes for a more peaceful life for the hummingbirds. On the other hand, the consumption and dispersal of the pine seeds by mice and jays is reduced, leading to an increase in pine seedlings.[12] Noise can therefore change interactions between species in an indirect manner and affect ecological processes such as pollination and the success rate of germination and, consequently, in the long term, it has an impact on local vegetation. This case, along with other terrestrial and maritime examples, illustrates the complexity of the indirect effects of noise on a natural system in which ecological interactions associated with predation, feeding or reproduction can be modified in one direction or another.

 Humans and other living creatures are subject to the same sound aggressions. The noise we generate, which disturbs non-human animals, also has disastrous consequences in our own lives. Noise has a social cost of 147 billion euros per year in France.[13] It is therefore of vital importance to consider noise as a problem of public health, veterinary health and ecological health, in line with the concept of 'one health'[14] in which human, animal and environmental health are no longer regarded as separate issues given how strongly they are linked together.[15] It is urgent to understand that the health of one individual depends on that of others and that human medicine, veterinary medicine and ecology must therefore share and collaborate.

What choices are there for the non-human animals who cannot, like us, isolate themselves *a minima* from the assaults of noise by resorting to walls and headphones? The solution most frequently cited is adaptation: 'Animals adapt very quickly.' Adaptation is a misguided concept which assumes that animal life will be able to find a rapid solution to external changes. In reality, such responses – we generally speak in terms such as plasticity or flexibility – usually come at a cost and have limited impact.

Animals react to noise with strategies involving avoidance or flight.[16] Moving away from noise in an effort to protect themselves is an initial possibility. Adjusting timings by singing before or after a noise can reduce disturbance to some extent. So, for example, several species of birds begin their dawn chorus a little earlier when their nests are close to airports, as a way of partially avoiding the rumbling of take-offs and landings. On another time scale, tropical crickets stop stridulating when lorries go past on a nearby road. Moving to a different space is another way of escaping noise. Roads have a devastating effect on animal populations since they fragment habitats, interrupt migration routes and, of course, kill accidentally. But they also have an impact in terms of sound, since traffic produces a significant noise level which disturbs animals, notably birds once again, but also amphibians and insects. So, for example, there is evidence of a reduction in the diversity and abundance of species in areas near tarmacked road surfaces. Evidently animals disturbed by engine noise are moving further away from roads.

Flight is not, however, always the most effective solution. Sometimes resistance is called for and the enemy must be confronted. In such circumstances it is a case of making yourself heard as best you can: singing louder than the motorway in the case of nightingales (*Luscinia megarhynchos*), singing higher above lowly city-dwellers like great tits (*Parus major*), singing longer and more often like chaffinches (*Fingilla coelebs*), singing faster like the two-striped grass frog or Taipei grass frog (*Hylarana taipehensis*), or singing immediately noise ceases as cotton-top tamarins (*Saguinus oedipus*) have learned to do. Birds, frogs, insects and mammals all demonstrate fight reactions but the battle is an unequal one and not without losses.

Whatever strategy is adopted, adaptation comes at an individual cost in energy terms and a shared cost in ecological terms. It is not always possible to move away, nor to sing higher, louder or for longer, or, on the contrary, to remain silent with the risk of then being unable to feed or reproduce. Noise is therefore a major threat to human and animal life. Noise is not the normal state for our environments. It is a toxic agent, a form of pollution. Just as we are polluting the air, the soil and the sea with chemical waste, we are also constantly allowing noise pollution to overflow from our windows and this can end up poisoning all living creatures. Noise should be regarded and treated as a form of pollution alongside chemical, light or radioactive pollution. Sound pollution should be addressed both collectively in local, national and environmental policies and individually in our everyday behaviour.

Anthropophony, the source of sound pollution, seems therefore to lurk behind every tree and under every stone. If noise is ubiquitous, how can we possibly find silence? Indeed, does silence even exist?

7
In the laboratory

Scientific careers are punctuated with periods of professional initiation. These might include learning to use complex equipment, travelling to far-flung places, international conferences, intimidating thesis defence presentations or crucial job applications. In the course of these adventures, spending a period of time in a laboratory in another country is a rite of passage. So, for example, young researchers often find themselves taking up a series of postdoctoral contracts covering a period of up to ten years of itinerant work. One of my three postdoctoral research posts was at the University of Bristol in the United Kingdom, where I was supposedly going to study the flight patterns of mosquitoes in reaction to sound stimuli. During my stay in England, I did not see so much as a single mosquito wing, but I did get to study the acoustics associated with the flight of the common green bottle fly (*Lucilia sericata*) – a very beautiful green fly – otherwise known in our rural areas under the appealing name of the dung fly. I also spent time analysing the subtle antennae movements of hoverflies, another group of wonderful flies masquerading as wasps, bees or hornets, and I enthusiastically measured the nano vibrations of the translucid tympani of Mediterranean cicadas transported, along with some goat's cheese, in a picnic icebox all the way from the hills so dear to Pagnol.

All these acoustic and biomechanical experiments were conducted in a very unusual space – a cellar within a cellar, a sealed and soundproofed chamber located inside a room, which was itself soundproofed, in the depths of a university basement. This isolation cell consisted of a small windowless room the size of the back of a utility truck. Shock absorbers blocked out the vibrations of footsteps and machines in the basement and thick honeycombed walls like the interior of a beehive absorbed any surrounding sound. This acoustic protection was the condition required in order to be able to take reliable measurements of very feeble amplitude with a Doppler laser vibrometer.

I spent many hours in this uncomfortable cubicle where silence and the occasional feeble buzzing of a fly reigned supreme. It was not an agreeable silence. Nor was time spent in these laboratory spaces, useful as they undoubtedly are from a scientific point of view, particularly pleasant. Sound was cut off to an extreme degree, the light was artificial and the only smells were either of metal or plastic.

I am not afraid of silence, nor do I fear isolation as long as I can get outside and into the fresh air. And yet I did not feel happy in the sterile silence of this underground container. I would enter it reluctantly, in spite of my longing to know exactly how a fly buzzes or a cicada hears. I would have much preferred to get outside and explore the slopes of the Avon gorge, far above the city, spending my time tracking down real, living specimens, chlorophyll, chitin, keratin and the solar photon.

A few years earlier, while I was studying for my thesis, I found myself working in a very different laboratory, this time in the Vaucluse, at the Harmas de Fabre, the home of Jean-Henri Fabre, remarkable narrator of natural history. Each day during my stay there I would read a section of his entomological memoirs. I remember being struck by this paragraph in particular: 'And then, my dear insects, if you cannot convince those good people, because you do not carry the weight of tedium, I, in my turn, will say to them: "You rip up the animal and I study it alive; you turn it into an object of horror and pity, whereas I cause it to be loved; you labour in a torture chamber and dissecting room, I make my observations under the blue sky to the song of the cicadas, you subject cell and protoplasm to chemical tests, I study instinct in its loftiest manifestations; you pry into death, I pry into life. . ."'[1]

Which is why I prefer the outdoors to any laboratory, museum collection or internet site crammed to the brim with animal noises. I prefer to record the song of cicadas rather than examine their dried bodies through a dissecting microscope. I prefer the silence of the outside world to the silence of the inside.

8

Absolute

Our lives – ours and theirs – are steeped in the sounds and noises which brush past us or collide with us at every moment. Might silence therefore be the total absence of sounds and of noises, an *absolute silence*, a sort of acoustic precipice where all vibrations perish without a cry?

We know that sound is a transitory phenomenon resulting from a movement defined within the parameters of amplitude, time, frequency and phase. If the intensity of this phenomenon is reduced to nothing, then sound does not exist. But what does a total absence of sound activity really mean? Is there such a thing as zero sound?

Airborne sound is essentially a movement of air particles. Sound activity can therefore be measured, in the first instance, as the distance particles travel or, in other words, how far they move in fractions of metres. It is also possible to estimate the speed and the acceleration of these particles. The more dynamic the particles become, the faster they move and the more energy they free into the air. This energy becomes sound power when it is expressed in units of time.

However, measurement of sound activity tends to refer to variations in atmospheric pressure which result from these movements of particles. The pressure of a gas depends on the mass and the acceleration of particles acting on a given surface. Sound only exists when the pressure produced is greater than atmospheric pressure at sea level, which equals 101,325 pascals (Pa). What is being measured therefore is not energy intensity but sound pressure level (SPL).

The level of sound pressure is not measured according to the pressure at sea level but according to our own auditory capacities. This self-reference requires notions of logarithmic scale and of relative intensity, which gave rise to the decibel (dB), familiar to us all given that they are indicated on the coloured labels of vacuum cleaners but often inadequately used and poorly understood. Admittedly this tool is extremely complex to assimilate; each time I need to use it, I find myself fondly recalling a remark made by an English physics colleague who, in the corridors of a Scottish university, was overheard declaring: *'I hate dBs!'*

The first change imposed by decibels is the switch from a linear scale to a logarithmic scale. Logarithms, in the plural since there are several of them (Napierian logarithms; decimal logarithms using base 10, also known as common logarithms; base 2 binary logarithms), are a wonderful mathematical invention handed down to us by the greatest mathematicians – John Napier, who first discovered them, and then, among others, Isaac Newton, Gottfried Leibniz, Jacques Bernoulli and Leonhard Euler.

Logarithms allow us to reduce amounts expressed over a very large range, going for example from a nano (+0.000000001) to a billion (+1,000,000,000) to numbers within a much more manageable range where the limits are set between −9 and +9 for a transformation into decimal logarithms. Revolutionary to the core, logarithms reduce differences by making the small things of this world bigger and the big things smaller.

This change does not happen without a certain amount of difficulty given that we measure the world in linear terms. The metric scales taught from our childhoods effectively all rely on regular scales and units: metres, kilos, litres, seconds and degrees Celsius. In reality, logarithms are all around us in the appearance and operation of biological systems: the spirals of a snail's shell or of a galaxy, the intensity of an earthquake, musical intervals, chemical and thermodynamic balances or the processes involved in the propagation of a pathogenic agent such as coronavirus.

Logarithms also shake up the laws of algebra since they enable multiplications to be transformed into additions, divisions into subtractions and powers to be expressed as multiplications. These properties of compression and computation explain why logarithms are used across all scientific domains, in all engineering applications and in the electronic systems which are all around us.

The ear can pick up sounds with very low and very high pressure, ranging from 0.00002 to 200 pascals at sea level. Since the order of magnitude is 20,000,000 (20 million) pascals, it is preferable to use a logarithmic scale to measure sound pressure. Given that the ear is generally considered to function only above a variation in pressure of 0.00002 Pa, it seems also logical to measure the level of sound pressure received against this reference threshold. The level of sound pressure expressed in decibels corresponds to twenty times the logarithm of the division between the pressure measured and the pressure of our auditory minimum. Imagine the sound of a tuning fork vibrating at 440 hertz, or in other words at the frequency of the musical note *A* on the third octave, which raises the atmospheric pressure to +0.2 Pa at 5 centimetres distance. The intensity of acoustic pressure will be $20 \times \log_{10} (0.2/0.00002)$, or in other words 80 decibels of sound pressure (or dB SPL) at 5 centimetres. Decibels are amusing in that the algebraic rules are different. We need to handle decibels carefully since they cannot be added, subtracted, multiplied or divided in the traditional way without resorting to some mathematical tricks.

Two sources of 80 dB SPL jointly generate a sound of 86 dB and not of 160 dB SPL.

Silence would therefore be a moment when sound pressure would be at 0 dB SPL; in other words, an atmospheric pressure below or equivalent to 101,325 + 0.00002 Pa. However, this reference pressure is valid only in the air for a frequency of 1,000 hertz, whereas the sensitivity of the human ear varies according to frequency and works best between 2,000 and 6,000 hertz. This figure of 1,000 hertz was chosen for the purpose of mathematical simplicity. We are in fact capable of picking up sounds below 101,325 + 0.00002 Pa as long as they vibrate at the right frequencies. Silence could pass below the fateful threshold of 0 dB and become negative. These benchmark figures for pressure and frequency in reality conceal a number of disparities since the auditory threshold varies from one individual to another and even during the course of our lives, as a consequence of accidents and ageing. Furthermore, the 0 dB is defined by default for air but this measurement makes no sense for water or for solids. The variation of reference pressure in fact goes from 0.00002 Pa in air to 0.000001 Pa in water. The 0 dB for air cannot therefore be compared with the 0 dB for water. Finally, there is quite simply no 0 dB for solids, making any definition of absolute silence in plants or in the ground impossible.

Given the nature of 0 dB, is it possible to experience it or to encounter it either inside or outside? Does 0 dB genuinely exist or is it merely a phantom, an imaginary place in the minds of physicists? Is there a place on the earth where the atmosphere is in a state of complete repose, where all sound sources have dried up? Is there even any justification in searching for such a place? What could be the interest of finding a place without sound, or in other words, a place without any movement, a zone of desolation where living creatures are absent or else reduced to total silence by some form of fatality like that described in Edgar Allan Poe's short story 'Silence'? In this piece, written in

1837, a demon describes an African country which is a mixture of desert and tropics, a desolate place teeming with terrifying sounds, a country inhabited by just one man, an individual in the grip of an anxiety provoked by solitude. The demon ends up imposing silence: 'Then I grew angry and cursed, with the curse of *silence*, the river, and the lilies, and the wind, and the forest, and the heaven, and the thunder, and the sighs of the water.'[1] This silence imposed on the elements and on all creatures, whether animal, vegetable or mineral, brings no comfort to the man who spirals from desolation to terror and makes his escape from this place which has now become inaudible and suffocating. Absolute silence is hell, a mortal silence.

Disregarding the noises made by our own bodies, where could we find a space capable of offering absolute silence and for how long? Noise is measured in periods ranging from a few milliseconds to up to twenty-four hours, but what would be the minimum amount of time required in order to be able to declare a particular site silent? A few seconds? A few minutes? Surely not as much as an hour? Intuitively we might envisage finding absolute silence for periods of a few dead minutes in distant and uninhabited spaces such as the ocean depths, the mountain summits or hot or cold deserts. And yet, on careful reflection, we would in fact be heading for disappointment since sound and noise are everywhere. The fact that these places are difficult to get to by no means makes them totally silent.

Oceans are perhaps the last place on earth in which to seek absolute silence given that they are full to the brim with the sound of waves breaking, the explosive snap of pistol shrimps, the grunting of fish, the whistling of marine mammals and the roar of industrial engines. You need only plunge your head under water to realize that the other world, the underwater world, is far from being a silent one.

At the other vertical extreme of our planet, the alpine peaks could perhaps be places of silence but the sounds of the valleys and of the alpine pastures can be heard even high in the mountains. The wind whistles across the rock faces and whips up the frozen snow with a sighing sound described by Roger Frisson-Roche in his novel *First on the Rope*: 'the snow was now swirling round the rocks, and mingled with the deep note of the wind was a high piercing wail, like the ceaseless rustling of paper; the whole mountain seemed to be moaning! This weird noise was made by the slabs of snow sliding steadily down the white-coated face.'[2] The mountain not only sends back the echo of our voices but also sings constantly, filling the white expanses with sound vibrations, sometimes violent in nature.

Absolute silence could exist in another cold zone, that of the polar regions, but here too winds displace the air and make even the harshest frozen landscape whistle. The American Far North is sadly polluted by human machines, including snowmobiles. So, for example, the soundscape of the Kenai National Wildlife Refuge near the town of Anchorage in Alaska, a subarctic area composed of humid coastal zones, boreal forests and alpine tundra, is composed of 84 per cent wind and 15 per cent mechanical noise produced by planes, compressors, cars and snowmobiles.[3] Absolute silence is not to be found in these northern regions, nor is it present at the southern extremity, in Antarctica, with the roaring of katabatic winds and the colonies of seals, penguins and other marine birds.

Entry into a warm desert region inevitably means a reduction in sound volume, but an even greater distance would need to be travelled, requiring a considerable investment, in order to get away from human sounds and out of reach of flight paths. And even then, the wind, yet again, makes the sand swirl and blow over the ergs and the regs and can even cause the dunes to sing in a long haunting moan.[4] In such places therefore, it is the sand, the dominant element, which is capable of breaking absolute silence. In a kind of role reversal, Paul Valéry saw silence like sand, which, once again, is not an emptiness but a sound: 'Listen to this delicate endless susurration which is silence. Hear what is heard when nothing is heard. All is gone under the sand of silence. The story of all my delights and desires is a dead city, erased and enlaced in desert cinder. But hear this lone far pure whistling, creating space, as if alone it existed, of itself, to its depth.'[5]

Sound is everywhere and there is no possibility of escaping it; just when we think that silence is absolute, there are always a few little traces of sound, as in this account by Maurice Genevoix, who, on the muddy hills of Éparges, in the Meuse region, experienced the ghastly clamour of trench warfare. When, suddenly, the weapons fell silent, sound ceased but did not die: 'There were moments of an almost absolute silence; then we heard, nearby, the sound of the rain dripping onto the carpet of dead leaves.'[6] Nature, in its simplest possible form of falling water, once again manifested itself as calm was restored.

In order to find absolute silence, we need to resort to trickery, to human ingenuity, since there will always be a drop of water falling on a dead leaf or a chainsaw ripping through the adrets and the ubacs. Man knows how to protect himself from noise and how to create an artificial absolute silence. Noise-cancelling headphones destroy noise, setting it against an antiphase sound in accordance with the simple principle $(+ x) + (- x) = 0$.[7] At this very moment, I am wearing a set of these headphones which means I cannot hear the radio in the adjoining room, or the lawnmower in the neighbouring garden. With my ears covered up by this helpful device, I am free to drift tranquilly, following the flow of my unrestrained thoughts, though still a long way from the shores of 0 dB. In reality, a great deal more needs to be done if we are to attain zero sound. For that purpose, rooms that are completely insulated and lined with anechoic material – foam moulded in dihedral shapes capable of eliminating any echo – have been constructed over the last decades in laboratories like the one where I worked in Bristol. In 2015, Microsoft constructed a soundproof room measuring about 36 square metres, enclosed in six concrete chambers and mounted on shock absorbers. The sound level within this sanctuary went down to −20.6 dB, well below 0 dB![8]

But in the end, what is the point of seeking absolute silence if it means finding yourself in the sterile innards of an underground room in an aseptic laboratory? Going outside, rather than being inside, is the very essence of a career as a naturalist. Silence is not a void, it is not zero but is in fact everything except noise, everything except what is disturbing, stressful and irritating.

Sometimes at home I find myself seeking out silence in order to be able to listen more carefully or to concentrate more fully, but I am aware that this involves a form of tyranny, a joint imposition which is not always fair, and that there is no point in seeking out absolute silence. Never again to hear a fly in flight is a desire that would be difficult to justify – let insects be free to fly. The vibration of their wings, chaotic as it sometimes can be, is a foretaste of the sounds of spring which comes long before the shrieks of swallows.

9

Natural

It seems quite simply then that silence is not what we thought: it is not a dead thing in a desert of sand, but a living, changing landscape filled with the murmur of animal lives, the vibration of mighty trees, the flow of rivers and the rush of winds. Silence, from the perspective of natural history, is not absolute silence fixed at 0 dB; to use a definition suggested by a nursery school child, 'silence is a sound which does not make a noise'.[1] Whether hidden away in the depths of forests, mountains, savannahs, deserts or the ocean bed, this sound silence is what I would call *natural silence*, a silence which is self-evident, a silence which belongs to nature.

On the cold slopes of the Chartreuse mountain range or deep in the warm Guyanese forest, I was alone, comfortably settled in this natural silence which made me feel as though I was totally in tune with the surrounding environment. In those two brief moments of isolation and quiet, in those natural silences which were in theory very different from each other, my breathing was shallow and I had the agreeable and intense sensation of being more than usually alive, like the feeling you get when you fall in love or when you are moved by a piece of music, when bodies and instruments vibrate in harmony.

According to the classification used by Bernie Krause, referred to above though without being specifically named, soundscapes can be divided into three main groups: biophony, which includes all biotic sounds ranging from the faint stridulation of an insect to the deep whistling calls of a whale; geophony, which covers abiotic but natural sounds like the flow of a river or the breaking of waves; and anthropophony, which groups together all human-generated sounds. Natural silence can therefore be defined using the simple arithmetical formula:

$$\text{natural silence} = (\text{biophony} + \text{geophony}) - \text{anthropophony}$$

In order to attain natural silence, we need therefore to exclude any noises of human origin. Natural silence can only be heard where there is human silence, as the audio-naturalist Fernand Deroussen so aptly and poetically put it during a three-month period spent recording the resurgence of nature in the Haut-Diois, a natural landscape freed from the vibrations of aeroplanes and car engines as a result of the Covid lockdown in spring 2020.[2]

Silence is not an empty space, a void, but a fullness. It is a space where all the animals can wander freely, where they can communicate unimpeded, far from the chaotic commotion of human beings. Yet this definition cannot be a totally exclusive one. Man, if he so desires, is welcome in this silence. He need only allow himself to enter into complicity with the soundscape, to be a discreet presence, to accept a simple folding seat somewhere in the wings.

Three temporary conditions seem to be required in order for man to find natural silence – a suitably remote location, solitude and stillness.

A remote location is the most obvious of these conditions. You have to get out of your bed, out of your room, out of your home and head out along a road, then a lane, then a path or a forest track, and then, and this is perhaps the most difficult part, abandon any trace of human presence and turn abruptly off the main track to plunge through roots and branches.

I remember one occasion in Guiana on Highway 2, which leads to Saint-Georges-de-l'Oyapock, an extraordinary little town on the border with Brazil. I was following Pierre-Michel Forget, a specialist in tropical ecology, and we were looking for trees of the Virola genus, a source of fruits for the red-billed toucan (*Rhamphastos tucanus*) which we were tracking by recording their soft grating cries. Leaving behind the burning tarmac of the road – closely patrolled by the local police, customs officers and the Foreign Legion – we headed directly, and in a perfectly straight line, into the shadow of the forest, pushing our way through a thick jumble of roadside secondary vegetation: a dense curtain of plants including the alarming razor grass (*Scleria secans*), which leaves its distinctive marks on the skin. In the space of just a few strides, we went from grey to green, and, very quickly, from the noise of the road to the natural silence of the tropical forest. I would probably not have gone through that wall of vegetation had it not been for Pierre-Michel's experience. Sometimes you need a guide to help you get to these remote spots, at least in the early stages. Entering this other world is no easy matter.

It is not enough, however, simply to turn your back on human activity and step into an area which is uninhabited and rarely visited. You must also make a chronological shift and be prepared to choose a less obvious time of day. The ideal is certainly to go out when it is misty and cool since it is at dusk and dawn that activity is at its most intense. The middle of the night and the height of the day, midnight and midday, are best avoided since these tend to be quiet times when the voices of nature are silenced and also when there is often the risk of it being too hot or perhaps too cold. It is in the changing morning light that the sounds of those yawning and preparing for sleep intercept the sounds of those rubbing their eyes as they wake up, and the same is true in the evening light. The result is a unique acoustic dynamic constantly filled with new sounds.

The absence of light favours sound communication as sound replaces the movements and the colours of the body. Most of the earth's great singers are nocturnal: crickets, grasshoppers, moths, owls, nightjars, bats, frogs, tree frogs, toads, deer, cats, canids, and many others besides. But who takes the trouble to listen to them? 'The night, a "true night", how many men now know what it is really like? The waters and the earth, and the return of silence', as Albert Camus describes in his *Notebooks*.[3]

Finding a remote spot both in terms of space and time requires a genuine effort, since setting off from your hut in search of the unfamiliar, even unknown, is far from straightforward. Any such excursion is all the more daunting if undertaken alone, and yet such solitude is absolutely essential.

Setting off with other people generates courage, high spirits and enthusiasm, but it is impossible to listen or to record if you are not alone. The slightest movement or somebody whispering and everything is spoiled. I have very often had the experience of exploring sound with naturalist colleagues whose interests lay in different directions to mine – some were fascinated by plants, others by insects or frogs – and even sometimes with those who listened in the same way as I did. It simply never worked. We are so sociable, so keen to communicate, that we cannot stop ourselves from speaking, from signalling to each other. We simply do not know how to be totally discreet, we get in each other's way, and, most importantly, we are quickly spotted, smelled and heard by the very creatures we are attempting to record. We need to be on our own, find a remote space and choose a suitable time, settle into a temporary exile, keep our own company and sever all means of communication if we are to successfully observe the communication of other creatures.

Silence can only be encountered if any others present are themselves silent and if we are at peace with ourselves: 'I need people to keep silent around me. I need living beings to be silent so that the fearful turmoil in my heart can also come to an end', to cite Camus once again.[4] Solitude therefore implies a certain egoism which could be misinterpreted as a form of misanthropy – avoiding others in order to find natural silence. In reality, observation of nature, whether acoustic or other, is a biotropism, a tendency to focus on the living. All the naturalist's senses are directed towards the outside and these senses are only protected if they are not subject to distraction. Solitude is the prerogative of kings, of poets and of naturalists. We have only to think of Jean-Henri Fabre choosing to shut himself away in his 'Harmas' in the Vaucluse from where he could observe the behaviour of thousands of insects; of Jean-Jacques Rousseau who studied plants in solitude in the countryside around Ermenonville: 'Is it any surprise that I love solitude? I see only animosity on men's faces, and nature always smiles at me';[5] of Henry David Thoreau who immersed himself in frozen nature in the area surrounding his cabin in Walden Woods, Connecticut; of Theodore Monod who, on his own and with remarkable tenacity, spent many years surveying the Mauritanian sand dunes in quest of meteorites; of John Muir who climbed the rocks and glaciers of Yosemite, alone and bare armed; of Dian Fossey, nicknamed 'the woman who lives alone on the mountain', who studied gorillas in the Rwandan forest. Even those naturalists who led major expeditions in the nineteenth century – Alexander von Humbolt, Charles Darwin or Alfred Russel Wallace – preferred solitude. Because of its ephemeral nature, the solitude of the naturalist is a blessing rather than a curse and is an essential element in the acquisition of knowledge.

Being alone in a remote place is not always enough – you must also keep perfectly still. Any movement, sometimes simply that of breathing, is a sign of life, a friction capable of being transformed into a detectable sound which can then act as an alarm and trigger changes in the immediate living environment. As far as possible, we need to focus on making sure our body is not disturbing the soundscape, that it is not affecting the behaviour of the animals which occupy the space into which we have intruded. When I was studying the song of the cicada, I remember not moving except to press the recording button of my tape recorder. The cicadas, initially some distance away, stopped noticing me and gradually came closer, even landing on my arms. By keeping still, we need to give animals the chance to forget all about us and get on with their daily lives with no constraints except those they bring themselves.

So, find yourself a remote spot where you can be alone, keep perfectly still in order to observe, listen and sometimes record, and do nothing else; like Walt Whitman who wrote: 'Now I will do nothing but listen,/ To accrue what I hear into this song, to let sounds contribute/ toward it.'[6] This state is a form of meditation in which you are alone with the songs and cries of animals and the silence of your own thoughts. But, unlike the practice of meditation, the naturalist's period of exploration is an act focused on the external rather than the internal, a time to forget personal matters and to tune in to the sound of nature breathing rather than concentrating on your own breath. This period of concentration can be, on the one hand, objective and scientific and, on the other, subjective and contemplative. It is a form of observation defined by the principles of scientific rigour and, at the same time, a vibrant individual experience which will almost certainly become a moving memory.

Given the right conditions, it is possible to find ourselves in the midst of natural silence. This silence – and we will see many others – far from being empty and dead is multifaceted and myriad, vibrant and living. It is a 'silence made of a thousand silences',[7] as Antoine de Saint-Exupéry said, or rather a silence made of a thousand sounds which do not make any noise.

Natural silence is found in a soundscape without anthropophony, without noise. Both the term and the concept of soundscape were defined in the 1960s by Raymond Murray Schafer.[8] The term covers all the sounds which can be heard in a given space and time. In this case, the perception is essentially from a human perspective since Schafer listens to the world as a musician rather than an ecologist. Schafer recognized hi-fi soundscapes which, like a system of audiophile sound reproduction, present a high signal-to-noise ratio; in other words, one where there is very little pollution from external sources. Low-fi soundscapes, on the other hand, are characterized by a low signal-to-noise ratio where sounds are drowned out by other noises. Hi-fi soundscapes are structured, clear and capable of being broken down into separate elements, whereas low-fi soundscapes are blurred, unclear and difficult to discern. Typically, night soundscapes, well away from human activity, are hi-fi soundscapes made up of clear sounds which can easily be detected and distinguished by the human ear, whereas daytime urban soundscapes are low-fi soundscapes made up of overlapping sounds and noises. Natural silence can therefore only be found in hi-fi soundscapes.

Schafer's definition of a soundscape accords crucial importance to human listening since the landscape in question is whatever is heard by man. We might therefore wonder if the soundscape only exists through the act of listening, which would in turn lead us to that very well-known thought experiment: 'If a tree falls in a forest and no one is around to hear it, does it make a sound?' – a question which could be reworked as 'Does the blackbird's song exist if no one hears it?', or 'Does a soundscape exist if no one is listening to it?' This question suggests that sound, whether it is signal or noise, does not exist without at least one human receptor, since otherwise it loses its meaning. But from a scientific and realist point of view – that of a physicist, an acoustician or a naturalist – sound exists even if no one is aware of it: the vibration of air, of water or of solid matter does indeed exist and it is not necessary for an ear to be involved for this vibration to be real. The idea that sound, or anything else, does not exist without a human presence is a very anthropocentric approach. Let us expand the exercise to include any form of receptor, so that the question becomes instead: 'If a tree falls in a forest and no living being is around to hear it, does it make a sound?' In that case, what would the scientific position be? Once again, it seems unreasonable to cast doubt on the existence of this sound, and therefore of the tree, even if no living being was there to observe it. The tree, its fall and the ensuing sound certainly exist physically. What about the silence then, notably that following the fall of the tree which has frozen all surrounding life? What happens if we shift the exercise to an absurd level by asking: 'Does a motionless tree make silence if no one hears it?' Realistically, the answer should remain the same: silence exists even if no one enjoys it. Without any movements audible to man or to any biological organism, the tree and the silence surrounding it are nevertheless still alive and significant.

For a number of years now, we have been able to record nature without being present ourselves thanks to automatic recording systems which do the job for us. In carefully chosen locations, we install little green boxes equipped with microphones. We programme them and switch them on and then leave them to observe in our absence like little spies. These sound traps, as some call them, are in remote places, positioned well away from any other such devices, and immobile – they therefore fulfil the three conditions required for an encounter with natural silence.

Such devices record a very wide variety of sounds without any one being there to hear them, and the microphones provide electronic proof of the existence of the sounds of birds flying and of trees falling. This audio evidence, in the form of espionage files, captures true natural silence with all its components: a crescendo of birdsong, trilling frogs, the harmonious call of whales, choirs of mammals, insect rhythms and, mixed in with all these, perhaps, pastoral silence and musical silence.

10

Pleyel

When I was a teenager, I was fortunate enough to have parents who regularly bought a season ticket for the classical music programme at the Salle Pleyel. It was here then, in this slightly dated auditorium in the elegant *quartiers* of Paris, at a time when the avenues were still cobbled and echoing, that I encountered for the first time the physical power of symphonic sound and the exhilarating effects of the combined force of the instruments. The whole experience is one of pure emotion: your breath comes fast, your skin tingles and your entire being feels uplifted. These sensations are clearly very close to the ones I experienced some years later during my encounters with natural silence, though in circumstances that could scarcely be more different. In one case, a remote location, solitude, stillness; in the other, a shared experience in a room crowded with other people and full of movement.

    I remember the beginning of one winter concert, perhaps Rachmaninov, sitting comfortably between my mother and a stranger. After a few moments' wait, the musicians (whom I admired more than anything else, or at least as much as cicadas and toucans) took up their places in a slightly chaotic manner, discreetly breaking off the discussions they had been having off stage and adjusting their chairs and music stands by a few centimetres, the accompanying scraping sounds on the polished wood floor providing a foretaste of the acoustic quality of the room. Then the first violin began tuning up, giving the *A* to the awaiting orchestra. Finally, to a round of applause, the pianist and the conductor made their entry, making a quick but elegant bow and taking up their places. Then the whole room, musicians and spectators alike, seemed to freeze for the space of a short, intense moment of concentrated silence and contemplation, before the vast wave of the orchestra unfurled and filled the room at the first movement of the conductor's baton.

On the occasion in question, I was wearing a Swiss watch, a birthday present I had received a few months earlier. The second hand of this relatively cheap brand was somewhat noisy. These watches mark the seconds with a clearly audible click which is in fact difficult to ignore. At the second bar, the lady to my right made it clear, politely but firmly, that I should remove my watch, since the regular ticking sound was offensive to her music-loving ear. With all the force of my thirteen-year-old self I felt somewhat irritated that this strict lady was issuing me orders from the starboard while the maternal authority was clearly on the port side, but I obeyed and hid the offending object deep in the pocket of my neatly ironed trousers.

Today, I perfectly understand the request made by this listener. Clearly the noise, however minuscule, had to be removed in order to give unimpeded access to the music. More than thirty years later, I have myself become an elderly lady exasperated by other people's noises. The irritating noises of my daily life are countless: cars, aeroplanes, lawnmowers, excavators, radios, televisions, telephones, portable speakers, dishwashers, washing machines, fridges and, of course, sometimes clocks and watches.

This musical memory might suggest that I am a musician. To my great regret, I never received any musical education. I did not study musical theory and I did not learn to play an instrument. To make up for this deficiency, I am now studying the classical guitar, as a hobby, in the first instance by discreetly following the lessons of my eldest child, and then gradually becoming her pupil. As I have a limited sense of time and of rhythm, I frequently massacre the quavers, leaps, syncopations and triplets, and I am particularly poor at managing all the pauses and silences. 'But Dad, didn't you see there was a silence there?' Silence can therefore be seen and can be transcribed other than by the sequence of letters *s-i-l-e-n-c-e*. But how do we write silence in music?

I have discovered, therefore, that the longest musical silence is the rest symbol, which lasts for eight quarter notes or crotchets, but which can be extended by a length of time equivalent to the number specified above it. Silence is also a black square, a solid, inert mass which seems too heavy for the five delicate lines of the stave. The whole rest and the half rest, symbols mostly seen in musical scores, are somewhat slimmer rectangles, the whole rest like a bat clinging on the *D* and the half rest like a mouse perched on the *B*, two mammals, one on the ceiling, the other on the floor, both of them well-behaved and silent.

Fascinated by how music is written and by the graphic beauty of musical scores, whether manuscripts by Mozart or those generated by a machine, I like to imagine what would happen if a tiny bit of confusion was introduced into such an ancient mechanism. What would happen if you moved the rest and the half rest on the stave? What would be the effect if you attached a rest to the *F* sharp or the *F* flat? What would it mean if a half rest was placed on the *E* flat or on the *E* sharp? Does musical silence have a pitch? Is it an *F*, an *E* or a *D*? The rests and half rests and other brief pauses for breath are the grapes clinging to the trellis of the score, spreading out over several lines of the stave, like silent chords. The shorter and darker the silence, the more grapes of silence are needed in order to describe it.

Since silence is a sound which makes no noise, perhaps in music too it is a note which is not sounded.

11

Music!

Given that man 'copied the forms of his hunting and industrial implements from beaks, teeth and claws' and 'from fruits he borrowed their forms for his first pots', that 'his awls and needles were at first thorns and fishbones',[1] and that clearly his first artistic attempts on cave walls represented the fauna and flora of his immediate environment, it seems reasonable to suppose that his first musical attempts, whether vocal or instrumental, were reproductions of natural sounds. It is highly likely that the sounds coming from savannahs or forests helped create human music by imitation or by the direct inclusion of patterns which were to some extent melodic. This inspiration from the outside world suggests the existence of a certain musicality in birdsong, in the whistling of the wind, in the eddies of a river or in the stridulations of an insect.[2]

Raymond Murray Schafer, whose work on soundscapes I have mentioned above, indirectly supports this idea of original musical inspiration since he perceives the world of sound 'as a microcosmic musical composition'. Schafer refers in particular to the ideas of the American musician John Cage, who considered music as 'sounds, sounds around us whether we're in or out of concert halls'. Schafer takes this definition of music a step further, declaring: 'Today all sounds belong to a continuous field of possibilities lying within the comprehensive dominion of music.'[3] The sounds of nature, along with those of human machines, are therefore, by default, musical sounds. The nightingale's song and the sound of a train can be included in a musical composition, with or without modification, as long as it is accepted that the work in question does not follow the dictates of western, or so-called classical, composition. Pierre Schaeffer – be careful of the homophony of these surnames – transforms these sounds which do not come from musical instruments into the sound objects of the concrete music which he created almost twenty-five years before Schafer outlined the concept of soundscapes.[4]

As soon as conversation turns to the links between music and nature, mention is inevitably made of the name of Olivier Messiaen, who transcribed birdsong to compose his *Catalogue d'oiseaux* for the piano: 'For me the only real music has always existed in the sounds of nature. The harmony of wind in trees, the rhythm of waves on the sea, the timbre of raindrops, of breaking branches, of stone struck together, the different cries of animals are the true music.'[5] François-Bernard Mâche, a pupil of Messiaen and a member of Schaeffer's group, was the first to integrate the sounds of nature, untransformed, into his compositions, notably in *Prelude* (1959), which includes recordings of the croaking of North American amphibians provided by Cornell University, a centre for bioacoustic research. Mâche introduced *zoomusicology* – the search for musical values in animal sounds.[6] So many artists have followed in the footsteps of Mâche and included animal sounds in their musical creations that it would be impossible to try to catalogue them. However, David Rothenberg, professor of philosophy and music at the New Jersey Institute of Technology, stands out from the crowd because of his writings and his improvised concerts with animals. Rothenberg established a very powerful connection between music and nature: 'I delve into the sound of nature because I know how much it can become like the sound of humanity.'[7] In each sound of nature, Rothenberg hears a human equivalent, and in the well-defined and repeated structure of animal songs, particularly those of the humpback whale (*Megaptera novaeangliae*) and the thrush nightingale (*Luscinia Luscinia*), he detects an even more powerful similarity with music than with human language, even though a parallel is often drawn between these two. Using the intermediary of his clarinet or saxophone, he manages to improvise interspecies music, playing alongside singing animals such as whales, birds and insects. Even without beat, harmonics or structure, Rothenberg detects musicality in the animal sounds that surround him and in return creates the animality of the notes he produces. One of his most powerful collaborations with animal choruses is his clarinet concert played in the midst of a teeming cloud of periodical cicadas (*Magicicada*, spp.).[8] These cicadas wait patiently for thirteen or seventeen years, not a single year more or less, buried in the ground in the form of white larvae, before transforming into a winged black adult with red eyes and invading American parks and rural areas in their billions. Their large-scale and highly synchronized emergence produces deafening soundscapes dominated by the intense chorus of males in search of their soulmate. Here Rothenberg positions himself at the centre of the collective chorus and finds his musical score amongst the cicadas excited by the imminent prospect of mating.

We can listen to cicadas and interact with them with the help of bioacoustic experiments in an attempt to try to understand exactly what it is they are singing, as did John Cooley and David Marshal from the University of Connecticut.[9] We can also listen to cicadas in order to identify musical overtones, and in this case we are engaging in an artistic form of listening and an artistic game in the manner of Rothenberg. Ideally, we would succeed in combining both approaches – scientific objectivism and artistic aestheticism – in a single pair of ears, a single brain. It is perhaps in this convergence of science and art that the richness of audiobiophilia, this scientific and aesthetic attraction to the sounds of nature, is to be found – a scientific point and a musical counterpoint.

Bernie Krause is another seminal figure in the mix between science and the arts (I shall describe my meeting with him in Paris later in the book). Having played with some of the biggest musicians of the 1960s, Krause definitively shifted his attention to the great natural spaces of the world in order to seek out musicality and highlight the extraordinary diversity of sounds produced by nature.

Krause and many other observers of soundscapes use musical metaphors to evoke the sounds of nature with references to animal musicians, the great animal orchestra, the animal symphony, animal scores and the concert of nature. Literary descriptions of animal sounds – and there are some examples in this book – almost always refer to musical terms, beginning with the word *song*, which does not in fact apply to the sound production of a great many species who, anatomically speaking, do not have vocal organs. But there are also references to *notes, melody, timbre, trill, duet, glissando, chorus, tempo* and many others. In reality, it is very difficult to avoid using musical vocabulary given that our vocabulary for the sounds of nature is poor in contrast with our rich vocabulary for music. But are there genuine convergences in sound terms between animals and western musical compositions?

Scientific studies of animal musicality are thin on the ground and mostly focus on whales and birds. The humpback whale fascinates both scientists and musicians who hear in the rhythms of its vocalizations a musical prosody with potential in terms of composition and sound interactions.[10] Easily accessible to our ears, even in the heart of the city, birds have also inspired a great many poets and musicians. One bird reputed for its musicality is the aptly named musician wren (*Cyphorhinus arada*) found in the Amazon rainforest. This bird's song is fluting and structured in a regular succession of quavers and crotchets. The shifts in frequency between the syllables show consonances using intervals of fourths, fifths or octaves.[11] This song is so tonal that it inspired the Brazilian musician Heitor Villa-Lobos to write his symphonic poem *Uirapuru*, the name given to the musician wren in the Amazonian Tupi language, and also meant that Krause's recording fitted perfectly in the symphony *The Great Animal Orchestra: Symphony for Orchestra and Wild Soundscapes*, created along with the English composer Richard Blackford. Further north in the American continent, the hermit thrush (*Catharus guttatus*) sings with syllables made up of frequencies which are integer multiples; for example, the syllable B has a frequency which is twice as high as the syllable A. The notes produced by this bird are therefore harmonics of each other. However, the western diatonic major scale is constructed on the basis of the harmonic series, the root note and the third having, for example, shared harmonics.[12] This thrush, therefore, has a particular musical signature. The common potoo (*Nyctibius griseus*), a strange nocturnal bird found in South America, copied by the trombone in the symphony composed by Blackford and Krause, also sometimes produces a song which follows a scale in almost perfect pitch. Yet such convergences are rare and are generally the result of a random evolutionary process. The musicality which we convince ourselves we can detect is by no means always present, as in the case of that other wren, the northern nightingale wren (*Microcerculus philomela*), where, in spite of its musical-sounding name, vocalizations do not follow the harmonic rules of western music.[13]

The desire to find musicality in nature involves hearing an organization similar to that of a symphonic orchestra in the structure of natural soundscapes. This correlation essentially comes from the acoustic niche hypothesis proposed by Krause.[14] This theory, which I shall be referring to again at a later stage, suggests that each animal species in a landscape or sound environment occupies their own acoustic space in terms of amplitude, duration, frequency and phase without overlapping the acoustic niches of any other species who may be vocalizing at the same time. This species-by-species exclusivity results in a partitioning process (comparable to the creation of a musical score) being applied to animal species rather like that in a symphonic orchestra where each family of instruments occupies a particular place and plays a clearly defined role. This theory, elegant and attractive as it is, has been corroborated and refuted on many occasions. It cannot unfortunately be tested experimentally since it is the result of a slow co-evolution which is impossible to reproduce or modify by any manipulations *in natura*. The comparison with an orchestra is a delicate one, especially when, in other authors, we find references to the presence of a conductor who might possibly be divine.

In his book *Pourquoi la musique?* the philosopher Francis Wolff defines music in a very concise way as 'the art of sounds'. Birds organize their sounds and structure their vocal outpourings using rhythms and syntaxes and sometimes sing in duos, trios and choirs, but is their goal in doing so an artistic one? When, in 1910, Lolo the donkey, alias Joachim-Raphaël Boronali, painted *Et le soleil s'endormait sur l'Adriatique* using his tail, was he an artist? Did he have an artistic intention in painting this canvas? Certainly not. There is beauty in natural objects – the whorls of a composite flower, the spirals of an ammonite, the pattern of tree bark, the mosaics of insects' eyes. Yet a plant, a mollusc, an oak or a fly are not *a priori* artists. Singing animals lack the artistic intention that would allow them to be considered as musicians. Soundscapes lack the desire to please that would make them orchestras. We must not forget that the sounds produced by animals represent behaviours which are costly in energy terms and potentially dangerous, and that they come about as the result of natural selection and sexual selection. Sound is a key element in certain vital functions which are useful for reproduction, feeding, hunting or flight but it is in no sense produced with any artistic intention.

Nevertheless, Francis Wolff's definition of music introduces another, even more delicate, definition by raising the question – what is art? Wolff makes no attempt to evade this issue and sees art from the point of view of the receiver rather than from that of the producer: 'art is less something we do but more something we admire', regardless of whether the thing in question is popular or scholarly, simple or universal, whether it comforts or disturbs. Yet nature is capable of producing beauty and emotions. The song of nightingales, of whales, of crickets, or of natural landscapes provokes admiration and emotion, not only for us humans who cannot fail to notice the beauty inherent in all these sounds, but also for non-human animals. Animals are affected by the sounds of other animals which trigger a powerful sensory response and procure certain fundamental emotions: the attraction of one sex towards another on hearing a chorus of song, the antagonism felt towards a competitor's territorial song, the shock provoked by the cries of a prey, the fear when a predator's cry is detected.[15] Moreover, the acoustic emotions of animals and the musical emotions of humans follow similar neuronal processes, as has been suggested in the context of the white-throated sparrow (*Zonotrichia albicollis*).[16] So, yes, in these conditions, in this definition of music and of art, the sounds of nature, whatever they may be, whether the harmonic songs of endearing whales or the chaotic buzzing of dung flies, are all artistic expressions, animal music that can be listened to like arias. If nature does not necessarily follow the rules of music as taught in the conservatoire, it can still be listened to *as* music.

But if silence exists in nature and can take a number of different forms, as we have begun to discover, can it also exist in music? Without venturing into musical domains outside my area of knowledge, I would like to mention some remarkable musical silences.

The first of these is the radical silence of John Cage's *4′33″* composed in 1952 – four minutes and thirty-three seconds of silence and complete stillness on the part of the musicians. *4′33″* is, on the surface, an easy work to listen to and interpret, a piece accessible to all, music lovers or not. In reality quite the opposite is true. Imagine what would happen if you tried to interpret it with a group of friends or your family, outside, in a natural setting during a little stroll or a long hike? You might try to improvise a performance of *4′33″* by simply asking everyone to come to a halt, to stop talking, to slow down their thoughts, to let time stand still and concentrate their attention on external sounds. You might succeed for a few tens of seconds, but interpreting *4′33″* in a woodland or in a field is a genuine challenge. Perhaps it is already helpful just to suggest a minute's listening – not a minute's silence, which might have commemorative connotations – but a simple minute, just the introduction to *4′33″*. The idea is not about paying a sorrowful tribute to a nature in decline but simply about listening to the conversations of other living creatures in a musical work.

The second musical silence is a silence experienced in 1993 in the audience of the vast Parisian auditorium of Bercy during a concert by Paul McCartney, who at that time was once again performing the songs he had written with the Beatles. 'All My Loving' was one of the first songs recorded by the Liverpool group in 1963 on the album *With the Beatles*. The somewhat saccharine words are disconcertingly simple but the music is remarkably powerful. In a flawless staging, the group inserted a pause or interruption at the beginning of each chorus and of the bridge. In that moment of silence, that single beat in a 4/4 measure, that clever rest, everything – the musicians, the music and the audience – was as though held in suspense. The entire auditorium was in harmony, on the stage with the musicians for that single second of listening, where everything came to a halt, where the music seemed to hold its breath. Everyone was frozen in a shared silence, as though vibrating in unison. These silences act as acoustic incisions cutting up and structuring the piece. Without them, the song would fall flat and the screams of the fans would fade away. The same is true of the silences of certain animals such as those of cicadas, for example, where silences lasting just a few microseconds interrupt long scratchy sequences giving an extra dimension to these sometimes monotonous songs. The silence provides rhythm and breaks up the chirping sounds.

The other silences are in the context of classical music listened to via the internet and through a headset as a result of the Covid-19 lockdown. First of all, there are all those silences which precede symphonic music, those moments of concentration before the opening bars, but also the silences which come at the end of a piece of music, those final silences which bring us back to reality, to the lights and the sounds of the room, to the objects around us once our noses and ears have been disentangled from a telephone or a computer. So, for example, the Franco-Georgian artist Khatia Buniatishvili brought the *Concert for Piano in A minor* by Robert Schumann, interpreted by the Frankfurt Radio Symphony, to a dramatic end, extinguishing the music in a long silence and holding the entire room in a state of stillness for a few moments thanks to her hands held in suspense above the keys.[17] And then, there are also the silences at the heart of the music, silences which would perhaps have passed unnoticed were they not emphasized by the musicians. In Beethoven's *Piano Concerto no. 3*, the pianist Alice Sara Ott and Mikko Franck, the conductor of the Radio France Philharmonic Orchestra, imposed a frozen silence, not a pause in which to cough or to get into a more comfortable position on a creaking chair, but a musical silence which marked the passage from the first movement ending on a sombre *C* minor to the second movement beginning with a luminous *E* major.[18] This tense musical silence can also be found in the silences of animal choirs such as when a group of frogs ends their chorus on a fortissimo and starts up again on a pianissimo after a brief acoustic pause for breath. Finally, Satie's *Gnossiennes* seem steeped in silence. Here it is not a matter of silences written into the score but of *one* single complete and overarching silence which envelops and covers everything without affecting the music. It is a full musical silence like the natural silence of a summer's night. It is a silence rich in crickets and grasshoppers rubbing their wings together, in hooting owls and trembling leaves.

In this manner, the sounds of the earth do indeed form bridges connecting man and the living world through all-powerful music. All those works which bring together biophony, geophony and music allow the so-called barriers between nature and culture to be broken down.

12

Ourselves and others

This is the account of how all was in suspense, all calm, in silence; all motionless, still, and the expanse of the sky was empty. [...] nothing which could make a noise, nor anything which might move, or tremble, or could make noise in the sky. [...] There was only immobility and silence in the darkness, in the night. Only the creator, the Maker, Tepeu, Gucumatz, the Forefathers, were in the water surrounded with light. They were hidden under green and blue feathers.[1]

So opens the holy book *Popol Vuh*, which sets out the cosmogony of the K'iche' Mayas of Guatemala. Before there was any life, silence and stillness dominated, and amongst the gods present who would create the world was the plumed serpent, Q'uq'umatz for the Mayas, Quetzalcoatl for the Aztecs. The resplendent quetzal (*Pharomachrus mocinno*) is one of the incarnations of this god from the pre-Hispanic era. A magnificent bird, with its plumage of metallic green, iridescent blue, blood red and brilliant white, its trailing tail feathers swaying gently like a long train in the wind of the cloud forest, the quetzal symbolizes the freedom of an entire people. In Guatemala it is omnipresent – in local handicrafts, art, architecture, fashion, in the centre of the national flag, and even on banknotes since it is also the unit of currency.

In the winter of 2018, in the company of Thierry Aubin, a unique and remarkable researcher and the greatly admired father of bioacousticians in France, and guided by Pablo Bolaños, a biologist fascinated by his country's icon, we were fortunate enough to encounter this mythical bird of the high forests covering the volcanic foothills of Western Guatemala. These humid forests, known as cloud forest, take on a phantasmagorical aspect due to the wispy clouds clinging to the treetops. Though similar to tropical forests, they are by no means as warm, and it was therefore in autumn clothing that we set out to record the quetzal's song. Unlike its flamboyant plumage, the quetzal's song is a timid one, soft and haunting, wispy like the clouds that surround it. It consists of two alternate piercing rounded syllables, which are musical in that they are tonal and very close to a *D* and a *C*-sharp on the fifth octave. David Rothenberg would have had no difficulty in accompanying the quetzal on his clarinet.

We headed into the Refugio del Quetzal in San Marcos, a small nature reserve dedicated to this bird, not far from the aptly named town of Quetzaltenango. Each of us went off in separate directions in an attempt to record the myth. At some distance from each other, hidden, quiet and still, each of us was plunged into our own personal natural silence. In these moments of solitude, the external silence and the internal silence seem to collide. It is as though the brain is set free by the absence of movement and by a particular kind of inaction imposed by the expectation of the sighting. The mind is of course focused and turned towards the exterior with all the senses fully alert, but that does not prevent it from allowing the internal sounds to rise to the surface – all manner of different thoughts, some professional, some very personal, jostle together – clearly one person's internal silence is not the same as another's. Silence is at the same time a shared experience and a deeply individual story.

Finally, the bird made its appearance, trailing its feathers behind it like a banner. The first sound encounter with an animal is always an emotional one. You fumble with the buttons of the tape recorder, and end up setting the recording levels somewhat randomly, often, to your frustration, missing the very first sounds.

Further away, on the flanks of the Atitlán volcano where we had just installed automatic microphones to record the quetzal's call in our absence, and while we were examining the tea and coffee plantations which are gradually taking over the native forest, we suddenly found ourselves experiencing the full, untamed force of the volcanic chain on which we were sitting. Thirty-five kilometres away, the Fuego volcano is active and from its crater there erupted a dense, heavy sound which sent tremors through our frail bodies and shook the surrounding landscape. This burst of very low sound was almost inaudible to us since it was at the very limit of our auditive capacities and it felt as though we were experiencing it more through our chests than through our ears. This sound entered the silent zone of our auditory senses, just at the point where our too-small eardrums no longer vibrate in response to sound waves which are too powerful.

The explosion of a volcano is a low sound, the stridulation of an insect a high one. This is not a haiku but a reality which becomes more and more difficult to live with as we get older. A young person's hearing generally covers a range of between 20 and 20,000 hertz. Anything below this is infrasound, anything above it, ultrasound, the first too big and the second too small for our eardrums. With the ageing process, these frequency thresholds alter and the spectrum within which we are able to hear shrinks. High sounds become more and more difficult to hear and so a whole section of our hearing capacity is wiped out.[2] This hearing loss is known and expected but feared by musicians who turn up the volume on their sound systems and by biologists who, without realizing it, miss out on a whole range of species whose voices are simply too high.

My first long-dreaded encounter with this very personal silence happened in the garrigue area on the high ridges of the Massif des Maures, in the Var. At the time I was doing field work with Camille Desjonquères, a specialist in the acoustics of aquatic insects. Abandoning for a while the small pond which we had criss-crossed with hydrophones in order to capture the sounds of the little water boatman (*Micronceta scholtzi*), we set off on foot in the surrounding area to listen to the cicadas. Amongst the parasol pines, the cork oaks and the cistus there are numerous large and robust species of cicadas which are extremely vocal: the *cicada orni*, the large grey cicada (*Lyristes plebejus*), the black sorrow cicada (*Cicadatra alta*) and the *Tibicina quadrisignata*. But not all cicadas interrupt a siesta. Some species are discreet, difficult to spot and difficult to hear since they perch in the foliage of trees and produce a very high-pitched sound. This is the case, for example, with the pygmy cicada, *Tettigettula pygmea*, a little insect with a dark, hairy body, barely 2 centimetres long, with a chirping sound which is pitched very high, at around 16,000 hertz, not far off the critical 20,000 hertz. Although Camille spends a lot of time listening to water boatmen, she is less familiar with cicadas, but she lost no time in drawing my attention to a sound coming from the top of a pine tree which was, according to her, intense, rapid and constantly repeated. Following the direction in which Camille was pointing, I could see nothing and hear nothing. Even though she was adamant about what she could hear, and described the sound in detail, the insect only existed for her and not for me. She was in the zone of sound; I was in that of silence. I had to record in a state of blindness and deafness and examine the sound pattern of this chirping song on my computer before I could finally identify this little cicada, so familiar to me, so pretty and yet so cruel. I was horrified – old age had come crashing down on me through my ears and I knew that from that day onwards the reedy calls of cicadas would fade into the mistral. I can no longer describe the songs of tiny creatures, like the adorable *Cicadetta cantilatrix* found on the slopes above the river Seine in the *Vexin français* region, a very long way from the Mediterranean.[3] Farewell high-pitched sounds, hello silences – from that summer's day when the sky was so blue, so young, a piece of the garrigue was taken from me, suddenly so old.

13

To hear or not to hear

We have searched outside for absolute silence without managing to track down this 0 dB which does not really exist. Sometimes we encountered natural silence, that rich, full silence, free of human noise, and now we find ourselves confronted with something we were not looking for, something which is inflicted on us, in the form of *physiological silence*, the silence imposed by the properties of our own senses, a form of deafness which is a particular kind of silence, an individual silence, an inner silence.

In our encounters with the various worlds of sound, there is both the genuine absence of sounds and the perceived absence of sounds. A great many sounds dance freely around us even though we are quite incapable of noticing them since our hearing is limited in intensity, in frequency and in time. Sounds that are too loud are intolerable and capable of causing damage. Those that are too faint cannot be detected and are therefore a source of frustration. Sounds that are too low are infrasonic and those that are too high are ultrasonic. Sounds that are too fast are simply incomprehensible.

If we plot our auditory capacities on a graph where the horizontal axis represents frequencies in hertz and the vertical axis represents sound intensity in decibels, our comfort zone is represented in the form of a smile – along this curve between 20 and 20,000 hertz and between 0 and 120 decibels we are comfortable and happy. Anything outside that means pain or silence. But clearly these limits of audibility are extremely variable, changing throughout our lives, as a result of accidents and illness, and differing from one individual to another. My brother and sister do not have the same eyesight, smell, taste or hearing as I do. We do not hear in the same way and, of course, we do not listen with the same attention and the same interest. We can therefore easily find ourselves in situations similar to the one I experienced when trying to track down that irritating little cicada, audible to Camille but silent for me.

What is noise for some is not perceived as such by others and what is silence for some is not silence for others.

Our auditory status depends on our physiology, our psychology and our experience. Each one of us is, to some extent, hearing impaired since our bodies are not equipped to capture all sounds and all vibrations. There are sounds that are inaudible to us because they are outside the range of our auditory spectrum, but there is also a whole range of vibrations in environments we do not inhabit, or inhabit only temporarily and artificially, such as ponds, streams, rivers, seas and oceans, or plants, trees and different ground surfaces. All these sounds surround us, brush past us, caress us and perhaps even assault us and yet we remain unaware of them.

This partial human deafness is relatively easy to understand since it concerns us directly. We know that 0 dB and the bandwidth of 20–20,000 hertz are human attributes. But what about the listening windows of other living creatures? Do they operate in the same auditory space? Where are their limits of pain and silence?

The earth is considered to be home to around 8.7 million species even if this figure almost certainly underestimates the number of bacteria and archaea.[1] If we make the hypothesis that all arthropods and all vertebrates are able to capture sounds transmitted by air, water, ground surfaces or plants, the earth would be home to around 4.6 million species capable of hearing or, in other words, 53 per cent of global diversity. This proportion, very roughly calculated, is an extremely high one. Hearing does not therefore appear to be an exception and in this large number of species, in this diversity, each species is unique. So, for example, in crickets, species A and its sister species B can demonstrate very different limits of amplitude threshold, frequency response and temporal integration. In ethology as in ecology, it is better to refrain from applying a generalization made from an observation on a given species to any other species, even if they are close in evolutionary terms. Each species has its own sound sensitivity and its own physiological silence.

The 47 per cent of remaining species effectively have no knowledge either of sound, of noise or of silence. They live in total physiological silence. They have no more knowledge of the phenomenon of sound than we have of the sensation of magnetic forces.

Alongside species which are stone deaf, there are some species which were erroneously considered to be deaf because their ears are difficult to see and bear little resemblance to our own. In grasshoppers and crickets, the ears are located on the legs, in lacewings at the base of the wings, and in cicadas in the abdomen. Sometimes it is impossible to differentiate the ears from the rest of the body. Flies and mosquitoes have their ears located in their antennae and fish hear with the aid of their swim bladder, hidden within their internal organs.

Sometimes we are unable to identify any obvious organ capable of receiving sound, but observation and experiments indicate behaviours which strongly suggest the existence of a form of hearing in animals which were assumed to exist in a state of total physiological silence. This is the case for, amongst others, cephalopods, jellyfish, oysters, mussels, coral larvae or fish larvae, all of which have recently been proved to have a certain sensitivity to sounds.

Even earthworms – animals which sometimes inspire a certain amount of slimy disgust but which nevertheless have a crucial ecological role, revealed with such genius by Charles Darwin – seem to be sensitive to vibrations. This cannot exactly be described as hearing but rather as mechano-reception. Earthworms mount to the surface of the earth as their homes begin to vibrate when rain is drumming on the ground, for example. This behaviour appears to be a flight response similar to that triggered by the digging activities of moles, their principal predators, a hypothesis recently confirmed but already outlined, once again by Charles Darwin, at the end of the nineteenth century.[2] This flight behaviour is exploited by wood turtles (*Clemmys insculpta*) and by European herring gulls (*Larus argentatus*), both of which repeatedly stamp their feet on the ground, causing the worms, a tasty treat, to come up to the surface. Men have also learned to take advantage of this. In the United States, a metal sheet is rubbed across wooden stakes sunk into the ground causing these to vibrate and resulting in hundreds of worms rising to the surface which can then be harvested and sold.

Ears, that is to say peripheral systems, and brains, central systems, filter sound waves in different ways. This results in very different perceptions of sound environments and therefore of silences. For example, cicadas do not hear what we say because the human voice is too low – we are in their silence – but they do hear cars travelling over tarmac since the rubbing of the tyres produces a sound that is within frequencies to which they are sensitive. Men and mice have frequential audiograms which are very different, with very little overlap: we live in the same lodgings, sometimes begrudgingly, but we operate in virtually exclusive sound worlds in which our sounds and our silences scarcely ever coincide.

Silence is not simply a matter of an amplitude that is too weak or of frequencies which are out of range; it can also be a matter of timing. Animal songs draw their rhythm from the alternation of signals and silent pauses. Detecting these interruptions relies on the temporal resolution of receptive organs and on cognitive processes. The minimal duration of detectable silence, a form of auditory acuity, varies between species, as might be expected; it is, for example, 30–40 milliseconds in fish, 1–10 milliseconds in birds, 4–5 milliseconds in man, 2–3 milliseconds in bats and less than 1 millisecond in certain amphibians and insects. In theory, ears are not capable of detecting silences shorter than 2 milliseconds because the action potential – in other words, the variations in electrical current passing through the axons of neurones – have a duration and resting periods of at least 2 milliseconds. Nothing faster is possible. Nevertheless, the repetition of the signal containing these silences of less than 2 milliseconds and the triggering of a network of neurones, rather than a single neuron stimulated only once, enables this neurophysiological constraint to be bypassed thereby allowing extremely short silences to be detected.

All this shows us that certain animals hear and understand certain silences which pass completely unnoticed by others. If we listen to a European serin (*Serinus serinus*), the wild cousin of the caged canary, it sounds very agitated. This sensation of excitement comes from the fact that the human ear is incapable of following its song, which is a rush of notes crowded too closely together. If the serin's song is slowed down with sound analysis software it becomes clear that the song is in fact organized in trills and that the trills are made up of numerous syllables, themselves composed of different notes. The syllables are emitted at an average speed of 23 syllables per second and the notes are most often interspersed with pauses of only 3 milliseconds,[3] a period of silence accessible to birds[4] but outside the range of our auditory acuity. We are incapable of detecting the silences of the European serin and only by artificially slowing them down can we become aware of them.

We do not hear like birds and vice versa. Once again, the perception of sounds and of silences differs between living creatures. They do not have the same profile, the same flavour. In the same location, such as, for example, around the edges of a pond, the soundscape is not the same for the frog, the cricket and the bat. One of these may consider the environment as silent while the others do not. In order to understand the extent to which silences are relative, you need only go on a night expedition with a chiropterologist, those nocturnal and mysterious naturalists who are passionate about bats. They will lend you a bat detector which will enable you to hear ultrasonic sounds, and the night, which previously seemed silent, will suddenly be full of the rapid clicking noises produced by the bats' echolocation systems. You will, in a sense, be breaking into their sound space as though entering a new world and the glittering night will be transformed, making you aware that your silence is far from being theirs.

There are also a considerable number of species which were thought to be silent, and therefore mute, but which turn out not to be. Historically, the first example that comes to mind are the bats we have just gone looking for in the dead of night. Bats appeared to be silent until it was discovered that they were emitting sound in the ultrasonic sphere, in our physiological silence. The same is true for some of their prey, such as moths, and we have recently discovered that these whisper ultrasonic songs during courtship.[5] The field of ultrasounds conceals some marvellous surprises. Such as, for example, the fact that it was only in the 1970s that mice (*Mus musculus*) were discovered to produce ultrasonic sounds, and it was only more recently still that the diversity and complexity of these sounds emitted during courtship were fully understood, setting them on a par with those produced by singing birds.[6]

Other apparently mute species have also turned out to be capable of producing sound. So, for example, Chinese cicadas of the genus *Karenia* lack the abdominal tymbal mechanism which is the fundamental element of sound production in cicadas; in theory they cannot make themselves heard and yet they produce a clearly audible clicking sound during their encounters with sexual partners. These clicks and clacks are produced by striking their forewings against their bodies.[7] These cicadas are not mute, they simply use another acoustic method using organs not specifically dedicated to sound production. In birds, the greater rhea (*Rhea americana*), cousin of African ostriches, hardly passes unnoticed with its lofty 1.5 metres. All the chicks have a sound vocabulary but, at the age of seven weeks, they lose their vocal capacities, apparently as a result of a change in the shape of the trachea. Very recently, thanks to automatic recordings, rheas have been found to produce low booming sounds in the morning and the evening. These bursts of sound last around one second and occur at low frequencies in the region of 125 hertz.[8] The adult rhea is therefore not as mute as had previously been assumed.

Considerable caution needs to be exercised when claiming that certain living creatures are deaf or silent. We must be persistent in our efforts and ensure that the creatures in question are observed on numerous occasions in their natural conditions. This might involve testing them, examining them, combing through their fur, sifting through their feathers, parting their scales, turning them over, magnifying the details of their bodies, sometimes slicing them up under the dissecting microscope, or x-raying them with a particle accelerator, becoming acquainted with every anatomical detail in the search for a hearing organ; most importantly, we must forget our usual references, forget our own bodies, stop thinking in 'human' terms and accept that evolution has led to some very different solutions.

Physiological silence is therefore individual, with each individual living in their own silence and, of course, in their own sound space, their personal acoustic *Umwelt*. In 1934, Jakob von Uexküll, then professor at the University of Hamburg in Germany, wrote a book entitled *Streifzüge durch die Umwelten von Tieren und Menschen* (published in English under the title *A Foray into the World of Animals and Humans*) in which he introduced the notion of *Umwelt*, an idea developed and explained over the course of several dozen pages but ultimately a very simple concept to grasp. Each species lives in a sensory world defined by the properties of its receptor organs, one which is unique to that species and which therefore cannot easily be compared to that of other species.[9] The term *Umwelt* is difficult to translate and confusions with various other terms have marred the history of this concept.[10] We find, for example, a whole list of substantives (environment, world, milieu, space) qualified by a whole list of epithets (own, sensory, subjective, characteristic, individual, animal, specific) leading to twenty-eight possible combinations: own environment, own world, own milieu, own space, sensory environment and so on. If *Umwelt* is untranslatable why not simply include it in our own language?

The umwelt is therefore a personal representation of the immediate environment which is restricted by the sensory capacities and the lifestyle of the individual concerned. In the famous example chosen by Uexküll, the female adult tick, responsible for the transmission of Lyme disease, lives in an impoverished sensory world limited to a sensitivity to butyric acid given off by mammals, to the tactile contact with these same mammals and to an awareness of the heat they give out. These three sensory routes enable it to find a suitable host, feed and, finally, reproduce.

Each species, each individual, perceives its environment according to its sensory capacities, whether these are acoustic, optical, chemical, electrical or magnetic. These capacities can be highly developed or non-existent, and therefore sensitive or not to different forms of stimuli coming from the environment. The reception and interpretation of these stimuli form a unique representation of the environment, the umwelt, with its specific properties of detection, discrimination, recognition and interpretation. The tick's umwelt is clearly very different to that of humans or catfish, but my wife's umwelt is also different to mine for we do not have exactly the same sensory capacities: she has a strong sense of smell while I am almost anosmic, she is short-sighted while I am long-sighted.

Von Uexküll was not only interested in ticks but also investigated the sound aspect of umwelts through his studies of moths: 'the artful microscopic structure of the moth's hearing organ exists solely for this single high-pitched tone emitted by the bat. These moths are totally deaf to all else.'[11] The moths, some species of which have a tympan connected to a single sensory neurone, have a relatively broad auditory spectrum but this is limited to the ultrasonic field, where their enemies, the bats, operate. Given that auditory properties are very different from one species to the next and that concepts of signal, noise and silence are all relative, we live in very different acoustic umwelts and the acoustic environments we move around in have different timbres: the lows and the highs do not have the same density, durations vary, the distance sound travels does not have the same limits, variations in amplitude and frequency are not necessarily as contrasted.

If we are not in the same umwelts, how can we hear the bird's song in the same way the bird hears us? How can we listen in another's place, when we are separated by millions of years of divergent evolution? Even if we know about the filters of the tympans, the ascending neurones and the auditory nuclei, it seems, for the moment, impossible to get any real understanding of the acoustic umwelt of birds and other living creatures. We often think that our recording systems function like animal ears and that, indirectly, they represent different umwelts. But this is a mistake since microphones, amplifiers and recording devices constitute systems which have unique properties of sensitivity, frequency response, frequency sampling rates and levels of digitalization. They themselves filter the sounds they pick up. The recordings obtained are in reality probably more the reflections of the umwelts of electronic tools than of those of the living creatures we seek to understand. Often this can lead to false interpretations – the fact that the cicada sings as it does on this recording does not mean it perceives its own song in the same way. In reality, its tympan, its sensory neurones and its cerebral ganglions hear it very differently because they apply filters and frequency and temporal decomposers. The recording of signals does not reflect the umwelts of non-human animals.

Von Uexküll's ideas inspired a great deal of research, including in particular an article written in 1974 by the philosopher Thomas Nagel from Princeton University, with the now famous title 'What is it like to be a bat?'[12] – a question which could be reworded as 'What would it be like to hear the world as a bat hears it?' Thomas Nagel does not refer to the umwelt because he approaches the problem of access to others in a broader way using questions of objectivity, subjectivity and animal consciousness. He refers to the acoustic world of bats, whose ultrasonic echolocation system, although much described, analysed and experimented on over the last ten years, still remains largely inaccessible to human thinking. Nagel concludes his study by reflecting on the impossibility of being a bat and feeling what a bat feels, given that our imaginations are too limited and the bat's world is simply too far removed from our own. It is already difficult enough to put ourselves in the shoes of another human being, and consequently any attempt to become or to resemble a nocturnal animal who sleeps hanging upside down is quite simply beyond us. The animalization of the human being seems insurmountable.

Impossible as such a transfer may be, it is nevertheless worth trying, if only because any attempt to step into the umwelt of a bat or a moth obliges us to describe and understand this strange and unfamiliar umwelt. We need to keep expanding our knowledge through observations and experiments if we are to succeed in mapping out the limits of another creature's sensory experience, a process which is the only way we can try to imagine exactly what form these other umwelts might take. And even before that, we need to make sure that we cast off our *own* umwelt, discarding our feelings and our usual references. If we are to try to familiarize ourselves with other umwelts we must leave our own behind us and approach the new one with a sympathetic and open attitude. By doing so we will be taking a significant step forward in developing an attitude of respect for everything that lies outside our own experience, we will be slowing the tide of anthropocentrism whilst at the same time avoiding anthropomorphism. It may indeed prove impossible to try to *be* another but it is surely not impossible to understand that other, to gain an idea of what they hear and what they listen to, of the sounds which are attractive to them and those which repel them and, in doing so, share our songs and our silences.

14

At the museum

We are speaking on the phone for the first time. We do not know each other and neither of us has any idea about the face, size and build of the other person or about the space they occupy in a place we know nothing about – perhaps for him it is a Parisian living room overflowing with books, or a huge empty desk in a country house opened up the previous day in readiness for the coming summer. We know nothing about our mutual lives, nor about the paths each of us has travelled or how long it has taken to get to where we are. We are entirely focused on our conversation, absorbed in an acoustic guessing game with all our attention concentrated on listening attentively to an unknown voice coming from an unknown place. And yet everything goes well.

And then, in the middle of this long-distance conversation, there is a silence of a few seconds. This silence is, apparently, deliberate, like a friendly little challenge issued to me by my invisible interlocutor. Silence in a conversation is often experienced as a difficult moment, an awkwardness, a feeling of being ill at ease where bodies have to re-settle themselves, where eyes stop focusing on familiar objects and instead seek a solution further afield, as though the distant horizon could suddenly speak and bring this somewhat – though not entirely – static moment to an end.

Silences in conversations are rope bridges over the void where bodies and minds can quickly be overcome with vertigo. And yet, we learn how to cross them without looking down and from such experiences where we find ourselves feeling somewhat alone and tense, we emerge stronger, proud of having shared this suspended time. It as though we understand each other better, we read each other more easily and can therefore love each other without fear, whether it be fraternally or passionately.

But in our society silence is rare or else lasts only for a minute as a way of paying tribute or remembering. It is not done to be silent. Every second must be filled. Silence is a blank page in the middle of a book with a mysterious full stop placed in the centre.

On the other end of the silence, the man whom I do not know is Dominique Dupuy, a dancer and choreographer for whom silence has played a significant private and professional role. In August 1957, in Aix-les-Bains, along with his wife and five other dancers, he put on the ballet *Epithalame*, created by Deryk Mendel, an English choreographer and friend of Samuel Beckett, himself the author of a silent play called *Act Without Words*. *Epithalame* was based on the extraordinary *Quartet for the End of Time* composed for violin, cello, clarinet and piano by Olivier Messiaen, the famous transcriber of birdsong. Messiaen composed this liturgical piece while detained in a German prisoner-of-war camp in 1941. He considered this quartet as being destined solely for angels and not for dancers or other human beings no matter how sensitive and light-footed they might be. Messiaen therefore refused to allow Dupuy and his troupe to dance to his sacred composition. Since no substitute music could be found the solution proposed by the choreographers was simple and radical but also brilliant: the music would be replaced by silence. And so, as a result of a somewhat authoritarian ban, the first silent ballet was created, understood and loved.

Dances, whether classical in the opera, traditional in village squares or hip-hop in the city streets, whether performed individually or as a group, are always physical expressions of music where the movements and the rhythm seem as one. Yet the Dupuys dance in silence, without instruments or loudspeakers, with only the swish of clothing against skin, the muffled thump of feet on the dark planks of the stage floor and the breath of straining bodies. This dance without music would lead Dominique Dupuy to reflect at length on the importance of silence in our everyday and artistic lives. Since then, he has constantly questioned the place of silence in the theatre, in literature, the cinema, music and architecture.

He had, however, never had the opportunity to explore the silence of forests and oceans. In that phone call, he was asking me to consider a little performance centred around the importance of silence in natural history which he wanted to stage in the endangered and extinct species gallery in the Muséum national d'histoire naturelle in Paris. This long gallery runs along the north side of its older brother, the Grande Galerie de l'Évolution, a vast, high-ceilinged gallery, centrally located and teeming with sound where, under dazzling lights, a caravan of majestic animals is magnificently displayed. If the Grande Galerie de l'Évolution is the lay cathedral of evolutionary science, the endangered and extinct species gallery is its crypt, adjacent to it yet hidden and hushed, shrouded in mystery with its subdued lighting and the sombre message it contains.

If you open your eyes as wide as possible, muttering your apologies for making the wooden floor creak, you will find yourself surrounded with stuffed animals representing wild populations in critical danger of becoming extinct or, in some cases, already extinct and with no prospect of ever coming back. This is the case, for example, with the famous dodo (*Raphus cucullatus*) which greets visitors as they arrive, still somewhat bemused by the sudden change of lighting and dimension. This pigeon from the island of Mauritius is a most extraordinary looking creature: almost a metre high, with a stocky body like that of a hen, short wings that look like hands, a hooked beak resembling a bottle-opener and tiny eyes which seem to stare fixedly at you as though constantly asking the question 'Why?' Discovered at the end of the sixteenth century and subsequently wiped out as a result of human activity at the end of the seventeenth century, the dodo's coexistence with man was short and tragic. A single century of hunting and the introduction of exogenous species, a blink of an eye in geological time, was enough to cause its disappearance. Although sketches of the dodo were made by a number of travelling naturalists, we know very little about its behaviour.[1] Its song, or rather its cooing since it is after all a pigeon, was never clearly described, even if its name, do-do, probably given to it by Portuguese mariners, may have been onomatopoeic.[2] The dodo's silence is therefore, without exaggeration, a *silence of death*, a wake-up call reminding us of those who have disappeared from biodiversity. It tolls for all the silences of past species, those artificially wiped out by the hands of hungry humans and those gradually eroded by the climatic and cataclysmic crises which have occurred on the earth.

So, one Saturday night in September, we invited visitors to the museum to greet the dodo and to join us in this somewhat melancholy gallery. Thanks to the help of the Chaillot Théâtre national de la danse, everyone was equipped with an individual wireless headset enabling us to speak to them in total discretion without them being able to see us, and plunging them into a silence where even the sound of their footsteps and movements was wiped out. Perched on the fragile balcony which runs round the entire gallery, Dominique whispered to them the words of a Paul Éluard poem, 'A l'echelle animale' (On the animal scale): 'The forest there is the forest,/ Even in the darkness I see it,/ I touch it I know it,/ I go in search of the forest,/ It lights up of its own accord,/ with its shivers and its voices. . .'.[3] At the same time, I attempt to bring some colour to the specimens by talking about their acoustic lives now either in decline or no longer existing. We see our guests walking round, perhaps even dancing without choreography between the glass cases, silent in this very special place which, for a short time, belongs to us. Then, without a word, without a noise, all of them disappear as Éluard's poem comes to an end: 'I am with all the animals,/ so as to be forgotten amongst men.'

15

Past

Palaeontology reveals the morphology and the anatomy of the species which made up life on earth over the course of millions of years. Even if some of these species were absurdly large or strangely shaped, with unexpected protrusions or appendages like those found on the marine fauna of the Burgess Shale (mid-Cambrian period, −350 million years), thanks to artists' illustrations, museum reconstructions and digital animation films, it is relatively easy to imagine them feeding or moving around. From their bodies it is indeed possible to deduce a considerable amount of ecological and ethological information about, for example, how they moved around and the distances they covered, their diet and their likely place in the food chain, their chosen environments and their territories, their methods of reproduction and their rate of growth. Two major aspects nevertheless remain shrouded in mystery – their colours and the sounds which surrounded them. Since pigments are not conserved during fossilization, any attempt to describe the colour of a dinosaur's skin, a fish's scales or the integuments of insects from the past is likely to be more subjective than objective even if considerable progress has been made over recent years with the discovery of traces of broken-down pigments on birds' feathers or insects' bodies. As for sound, it is by nature ephemeral, appearing and disappearing and impossible to pin down. Knowing the sounds, and therefore the silences, of extinct species is a major challenge for palaeontology. How can we reconstitute the history of silence on earth? How can we know the composition of soundscapes whether terrestrial, marine or aquatic through the course of the various geological periods? How can we imagine the sounds of the distant past?

Analysis of the rare remains of vocal tracts such as the stridulatory mechanism of arthropods or the larynx or syrinx of vertebrates can provide some acoustic clues. However, any sound reconstitutions are risky since the physiology of the nerves and the muscles of such organs is completely unknown. The discovery and the descriptions of auditory systems, like the tympans of certain arthropods fossilized in amber or the ossicles of the middle ear of vertebrates, give us only minimal information on the hearing capacities of a few extinct species. We should not therefore rely too closely on fossils as a way of listening to the past. The most invaluable help certainly comes from phylogeny, that reconstruction of the lines of descent of existing species expressed in the form of a tree, sometimes complex in structure, where each leaf tip represents an existing species or fossil, the internal branches represent historic connections and the junction points or nodes indicate lines of descent. Phylogenetic trees enable us to turn back geological clocks and to formulate hypotheses on the appearance and the lives of flora and fauna from a previous era. By combining geology, palaeontology and phylogenetic reconstruction, we can therefore attempt to trace the major sound patterns of the past.[1]

Was the earth once silent? Did absolute silence exist at some point? It would appear unlikely. From the time the atmosphere was first formed – regardless of its chemical composition, its temperature and its pressure – and the oceans and the earth's crust first came into being – whatever their position, their forms and their locations – the earth resonated with geological sounds long before it echoed with the sounds of living creatures. Geophony – in other words, all the abiotic but natural sounds – is as old as the earth and includes the sounds made by volcanic eruptions, by the outpourings of lava, by the movement of water, of winds, of storms and oceans, the creaking of ice and the rumble of landslides.

In its infancy then, the earth was uniquely geophonic. Even if the first signs of multicellular life found at Franceville in Gabon date from the Proterozoic (−2.1 billion years), the first sounds attributed to living creatures probably came from ocean landscapes from the end of the Ediacaran (−635/−541 million years) inhabited by organisms made up of tissues of cells. These organisms, which are difficult to describe and class in known animal groups (metazoans), but which bear a certain resemblance to marine worms (annelids), sea urchins (echinoderms), sea anemones or jellyfish (cnidaria), could be benthic, bottom-dwelling, or pelagic, floating between the ocean floor and the surface of the water. With their soft bodies, these organisms probably did not produce sound intentionally, but their movements, however tiny, could generate vibrations and therefore underwater sounds. Moreover, starfish, sea urchins, bivalve molluscs and all their equivalents in present-day fauna produce sounds which are perfectly discernible and which form benthic soundscapes.[2] It is therefore reasonable to suppose that the ocean floors in these very ancient times were occupied by living creatures and were already generating sound.

The beginnings of biophony date from these enigmatic ocean-dwelling lives of the Ediacaran period which disappeared catastrophically or gradually – we do not know which[3] – and were replaced relatively soon afterwards, in the Cambrian (−541/−485 million years), by a new biotic of metazoans which, within some 60 million years – in other words in the space of about 20 minutes if the history of the earth was measured in terms of a single day – gave rise to present-day flora, fauna and mushrooms. Was this explosion of biodiversity, to use the time-honoured expression, of which the Burgess fauna is the symbol, also accompanied by an explosion of sounds? *A priori* this was not the case, since the first organisms of the Cambrian do not appear to have had any structures devoted to the production of sound. Even trilobites, which could perhaps have made a bit of an effort with their rigid exoskeleton so suited to friction, show no evidence of any rasp or plectrum which could have been used as a stridulatory device. Conversely, the diversity in terms of mobile species would imply the existence of incidental sounds caused by movements. For example, sea urchins, apparently so silent, probably generated sounds, though without doing so deliberately. These hairy animals are equipped with a single mouth apparatus, known under the poetic name of Aristotle's lantern and made up of five teeth which graze the ocean depths in search of plant or animal proteins. Just like the limpet with those denticles we have already heard scraping against the rocks, sea urchins can be heard during their breakfast and dinner times. Their skeleton, or test, acts as a resonator, amplifying the grinding sound made by their teeth. A group of sea urchins can constitute a veritable twilight chorus.[4] The sounds of sea urchins must therefore have existed as far back as the Ordovician (−485/−443 million years), the period in which these hedgehogs of the seas and the oceans probably first appeared.

However, we know of no Cambrian or Ordovician ears. Absolute silence was not necessarily present, but physiological silence was total and applied to all, except perhaps for the earliest jellyfish[5] and the first cephalopods,[6] which may have demonstrated a certain sensitivity or reactivity to sound, as observations on existing species appear to suggest.

The first to listen to the world were probably the agnathans – aquatic vertebrates without jaws, where the lateral line, this little row of modified scales which outlines the abdominal silhouette of existing specimens, could detect variations in water pressure and, therefore, probably, low-frequency sounds.

It was in the Silurian (−443/−419 million years) and the Devonian (−419/−359 million years) that the global underwater acoustic scene began to change. The first fish with jaws, whether they had cartilaginous skeletons (chondrichthyans) like today's sharks or bony skeletons (osteichthyes) like sardines, were equipped with true ears capable of listening to the surrounding sounds.

But, finally, why emerge from your individual silence? Why listen? Why seek to decode the world where the diversity of sounds is gradually increasing? What selective forces came into play and led to the first appearance of ears? The Darwinian response is so logical and so simple – survival. The ear, whatever its shape, its size, its operational mode, its position on the body, is a means of detecting prey and predators. The ear helps animals find food by picking up the uncontrolled sounds of other appetizing bodies rich in protein or, conversely, by detecting, sometimes in a fraction of a second, the movements of prowlers who are equally hungry. The ear quickly became an essential element of survival.

Hearing began therefore as a form of sensory surveillance, an attention focused on an entire environment from which tempting or alarming sounds could emerge. This auditory propensity to detect pointers for survival seems to be a deeply rooted atavism since it is still present in existing species, including man. Our ears are on permanent alert, listening out for the smallest change of sound which might indicate a modification in our immediate environment – a possible danger which jolts us to our senses, puts us on our guard and sets our hearts racing.

It is also possible that the first sounds heard and listened to were used for locating and intercepting members of the same species, notably within the context of encountering a sexual partner, though in the absence of any genuine act of communication. Hearing the other move can make it easier to find them and embrace them.

Under these waters which are beginning to teem with animal life, the early stages of intentional acoustic emissions may have come from crustaceans during the Silurian era. Using stridulation, these may have produced reflex rubbing sounds in response to being captured by a predator, such as a fish, for example. Trapped in the enemy's jaws and on the brink of death, the body of the prey reacts by contracting, trembling, vibrating and even sometimes producing hissing sounds. The direct transmission of the vibrations of the feeble and panic-stricken body of the prey to the powerful body of the predator can alter the outcome of the struggle. Astonished, shaken and seized with fear in turn, the predator abandons the prey, restoring it to freedom and to life. Which of us has not released a frog or a shrieking cicada we have managed to catch for the first time? The surprise of the vibrations, as though coming from a buzzer hidden in the palm of a child playing a practical joke, triggers a reflex which causes us to let go. The defence reaction of the vibrating prey undeniably brings an immediate evolutionary advantage which is then selected over the course of generations.

The paroxysmal sound reactions of struggling bodies were gradually transformed into the aggressive sounds of defence emitted by a prey *before* the final attack of the predator. These reactions, known as deimatic behaviour, indicate a form of intention and anticipation – their aim is to force the predator to back off by transferring the fear initially experienced by the prey back to the predator. These defence signals, which imply an auditory system in the predators, therefore function at a certain distance in that information is transmitted without contact between the two individuals. This marks the beginning of a certain form of sound-based communication which first manifested itself during the Carboniferous period (−359/−299 million years) under and above the water as biodiversity increased on emerging land masses. So, for example, the first amniotes, that is to say the first tetrapod animals where embryos developed in a protective liquid, would have blown or even whistled air at the approach of danger: the body, stricken with fear, rears up, puffing itself up and making itself appear bigger and stronger, then contracts and exhales, spitting out a sound of fear and anger like that of a cat which has the misfortune to cross paths with a dog. So, in 1877, observing the reaction of animals to pain and fear, Darwin wrote: 'Involuntary and purposeless contractions of the muscles of the chest and glottis [. . .] may have first given rise to the emission of vocal sounds.'[7]

A little later, in the Middle Permian period (−272/−260 million years) the first known crickets began to stridulate, gradually reducing the silence of the grasslands and forests of Pangaea, the supercontinent formed from the single piece of a future jigsaw puzzle. The first stridulatory organs were in place as early as the Guadalupian (−275/−260 million years) and perhaps marked the start, at least in insects, of true communication where it is in the interests of both the sender of the message and the receiver to break the silence – this is the beginning of sound-based courtship. The evolution of sound production and hearing in orthoptera – that is to say, crickets, grasshoppers and locusts – followed a number of different pathways and different kinetics, with stridulation appearing at the same time as hearing in some species or sequentially in others, but it seems highly likely that the sounds also appeared in the first place as the expression of a reaction to an ill-fated encounter with a predator and then, later on, in the context of behaviour associated with encountering a sexual partner.[8]

It was during the Triassic period (−252/−201 million years), following the major crisis of biodiversity at the end of the Permian, that the biophony really began to gain momentum, before reaching a peak in the Jurassic period (−201/−145 million years). Every possible space pullulated with life and the movements of all manner of creatures were accompanied with unintentional sounds – flying insects such as dragonflies or hymenoptera whirred around tetrapods including dinosaurs, with their heavy, noisy tread. Interspecies communication and intentional sounds developed in many different groups. Under the water, fish made grunting sounds and formed the first animal choruses. On land, grasshoppers and locusts joined with crickets and filled the night air with their stridulations. Stoneflies tapped their abdomens against the stones of streambeds. True bugs caused plants to vibrate while their aquatic cousins made ponds resonate with sound from the Upper Triassic onwards. Dinosaurs do not appear to have been very vocal, even though it is possible that, just like copulating turtles or snakes announcing their evil intentions for painful and even fatal bites, they may have made hissing or blowing noises and some of them may have been able to produce a honking sound thanks to strange cephalic protrusions.[9] It was in other tetrapods that sound first arrived and brought colour to the silence. The ancestors of amphibians, crocodiles, geckos, turtles, birds and present-day mammals were already making themselves heard in the Jurassic period. The first manifestation of sound in these groups occurred on a number of separate occasions and in independent ways, but it seems that most of the groups in question began to sing at night like the arthropods.[10] Night was, therefore, a driver in the emergence of sound communications. The absence of light restricted visual communication and the sound solution, which functioned even in total darkness, seemed an obvious one.

The large singing groups made up of mammals and birds were already active in these far-off times, around 200 million years ago. Largely nocturnal, certain species evolved towards diurnal behaviour, but even today the majority of animals essentially produce noise at night, at dusk and at dawn. Crickets, grasshoppers, amphibians, bats, cats and a great many other mammals only make noise at night. At the boundaries of terrestrial light, when the sun appears or disappears behind the horizon, geckos, birds, monkeys, deer and fish call together, sometimes forming loud choruses. Since man is diurnal, we tend to think that the other animals chat at the same time as us but, in reality, everything happens at night, when humans are in bed. Biophony – natural silence – was and still is essentially nocturnal rather than diurnal.

In the Cretaceous period (–145/–66 million years), the volume of the biophony increased with the diversification of arthropods and tetrapods. Birds were, of course, increasingly present on the acoustic stage. Insects moved around with varying degrees of discretion. They hunted, ran away, transported objects, constructed their homes and modified the environment to their advantage, generating sounds with each action. But, more than that, some of them expressed themselves through stridulation, chirping, tapping or vibrating. Their sexual or social communications made the entire planet vibrate.

Then, following a new crisis of biodiversity, known as the Cretaceous-Tertiary event, in which dinosaurs were wiped out but their descendants, notably the birds, survived, diversity of life once again grew richer during the Cenozoic, the last great geological era, which took us up to modern times (from –66 million years to our era). All groups in place diversified and, as a result, biophonic diversity increased. This was notably the case for birds and mammals, the major beneficiaries of the disappearance of non-avian dinosaurs. Mammals moved into new acoustic dimensions by producing high-frequency sounds. Certain rodents, bats and cetaceans created a marine and terrestrial ultrasonic biophony. These same animals also found channels of auto communication with sonar systems which enabled them to survey their environments using echolocation, a phenomenon which, in return, led to the evolution of ultrasonic hearing abilities in their prey, such as, for example, moths and lacewings.

Major acoustic changes came about at a considerably later stage with the arrival of modern men of the genus *Homo* in the Quaternary period (−2.58 million years). Whether they were *erectus, ergaster, antecessor, heidelbergnis, florensis, luzonensis, neanderthalensis* or *sapiens,* all these humans, wherever they were and however long they survived, produced sounds as a result of their activities and their communications. Their movements from one place to another, the first tool-making techniques, the first voices and music of *Homo neanderthalensis* and of *Homo sapiens* were probably not particularly loud and blended into the surrounding sounds. In its early stages, anthropophony was therefore simply a discrete part of the biophony. But the demographic and technical growth of *Homo sapiens* during the last millennia has meant that the sounds they produce have become increasingly powerful and dominant as tools became machines, voices multiplied and instruments turned into orchestras. Men filled the planet with their sounds and introduced anthropophony, and more particularly technophony, defined as the noise made by machines. The influence of sound rapidly become holistic, both on the land and under the sea. And so, noise was born, a form of pollution for man himself and for all other living creatures. Geophony and biophony lost ground, silence could no longer exist and everything was caught up in a maelstrom of sound.

So, throughout the geological ages, silence was by no means the norm. It declined over the course of the history of life. Geophony dominated the world for almost 4 million years and then, along came biophony with its triumphs and declines reflecting the various crises of biodiversity. Biophony was made up of incidental sounds caused by movements, of sound signals used by prey and predators alike, of reactions of fear and defence, of communication signals between well-intentioned members of the same species and finally of the sonar echoes of auto communication. These sounds did not follow on from each other according to a gradient of complexity but appeared, only sometimes to vanish again, on multiple occasions, in many different animal groups at different geological times. Like any representation of an evolutionary process, the sound chronology of the earth is not a frieze but a complex tree whose branches grow, split, cross, entangle and sometimes fall to the ground.

Today, modern anthropophony is in the process of dealing the final blow to natural silence. Human noise is imposing itself and wiping out millions of years of evolution and of sound diversity.

What will be the future for sound on earth? Predictions and science-fiction seem to ignore the acoustic element of possible and imaginary futures. But what will the soundscapes of tomorrow and beyond be like? How will the earth sound in a few years, centuries, millennia or even geological eras? What sounds will there be in the nights and days to come? Will anthropophony gradually decline and collapse or will it continue its hegemony?

16

Hiding

The battles fought between prey and predators are the result of long evolutionary processes which very often involve both sound and silence. The delicate balance between survival and action means each individual needs to make themselves as inconspicuous as possible so as to avoid being detected as a result of their scent, their gestures or colours and, of course, their sounds. It is in the interests of hunters and hunted alike to remain unheard. Potential prey must become one with silence in order to stay alive, to avoid being eaten, to keep starvation at bay. Since it is, in the end, a question of saving their own skin, prey and predators take refuge in a *survival silence* during moments of confrontation. This survival silence is neither absolute nor physiological – it is a circumstantial silence. For the prey, silence is a weapon of defence, for the predator it is a weapon of attack. In order to reduce to a minimum the sounds made by bodies once out of the safety of their hiding places, two possible options seem to be available. Physical morphology can be adapted by reducing incidental sounds, and vocalizations can be controlled by silencing intentional sounds – a case, therefore, of being both stealthy and mute at the same time.

Even before resorting to movement, morphology can help a prey melt into silence. For almost 60 million years, moths have been the favoured prey of bats, which hunt them using their sonar systems. The wings of moths, like those of butterflies, are covered with tiny scales and the arrangement and colours of these sometimes form patterns which are often extremely beautiful. These scales play a number of different biological roles – they are involved in the selection of sexual partners, they warn predators of potential toxicity and they ensure camouflage in the immediate environment. It has now become clear that these scales also have an additional function. In certain species, the ultrastructure of the scales is perforated, giving them a honeycomb-like appearance not dissimilar to the alveolar structures used in sound-absorbing materials to reduce echoes in radio or music studios. This wing covering helps to reduces the echoes of the sonar signals emitted by the bats.[1] The scales effectively increase the distance needed for the bats to locate the moths and therefore probably reduce the success rate of the mammals' hunting activities. In moths, the thorax is also covered with filamentous scales giving their backs a fibrous appearance.[2] These scales, which have shapes and patterns very different to those of the wings, also absorb the echoes from bat echolocation systems. This attenuation is very efficient, far more so than any fibrous materials used by humans. Shrouding yourself in a light veil of silence seems therefore to be an evolutionary response to the dangerous presence of bats, that is to say a slow response, evolved through generations and over the course of geological time. Morphological stealth tactics are nevertheless a passive solution given that the animal, in this case the moth, does not make any effort to be silent, but the structure of its body, modified by evolution, does the job for it. The search for silence can also be an active process and can be the outcome of an adapted behaviour, also selected by evolution.

The first stage probably involves avoiding making noise when moving around, and being careful not to rub against or collide with randomly placed objects. How many characters in novels, comic strips and films have given themselves away by treading on a dead branch? The same is true when it comes to non-human animals. They need to pay careful attention to where they step and how they move forward, pause, rest and set off again. They must avoid rustling leaves, displacing too much water or causing stones to roll down slopes.

The eastern deer mouse (*Peromyscus maniculatus*) is the prey of, amongst others, the weasel (*Mustela rixosa*), the coyote (*Canis latrans*), the American red fox (*Vulpes fulva*) and the barn owl (*Tyto alba*), all of which are endowed with auditory capacities which help them when hunting. Laboratory experiments have successfully demonstrated that the mice prefer to move around on damp ground rather than on dry surfaces and prefer a carpet of pine needles to one made up of branches and twigs. When possible, they also choose to move along fallen tree trunks rather than remaining in direct contact with the ground.[3] All these preferences indicate the choice of silent pathways – the damp substrate makes less noise than the dry one, pine needles are less brittle than branches, and tree trunks are paths free from the debris littering the ground surface. The mouse appears therefore to seek silence during its forays so as to avoid alerting predators to its presence.

Leaf litter insects, notably cockroaches and coleoptera, would benefit from avoiding the noisiest surfaces.[4] Like the eastern deer mouse in North America, an insect walking around on damp leaf litter generates less intense sounds than on a dry surface. Bare earth is quieter than grassy surfaces and leaf litter. Sand and bark are more discreet than leaf litter. On a silent substrate, an insect is detectable by a predator over an eight times larger distance, in a sixty-four times larger area and in a space seventy-two times greater in volume. The difference is far from negligible – seeking silence in a substrate brings considerable advantages. But safety is also in slowness: insects reduce their sounds by 3 to 8 decibels by reducing the speed of their movements. For a mouse, an insect, and undoubtedly for many other forms of prey, being stealthy evidently therefore requires precaution and care in choosing pathways and in the physical mechanics of the body.

The other solution for sound discretion, an even more logical and intuitive one, is to mute your own sound production. By simply keeping quiet the chance of being heard is reduced. This apparently self-evident behaviour is not however quite as straightforward as it seems, since cowering in silence means no longer being able to communicate, reproduce or seek help from parents. Remaining mute therefore has a direct advantage – that of not being spotted by the baddies – and an indirect cost – that of not being able to benefit from the presence of your loved ones. The result equates to a somewhat classical conflictual situation along the path of evolution, in this case a compromise between the need to be quiet and the need to express yourself. The equilibrium between two obligations is not necessarily the result of any rational process on the part of animal prey but is instead the outcome of long evolutionary processes.

Before opting to keep completely quiet, to be as silent as a Trappist monk, there is the option of trying to maintain communication but at a reduced volume. By lowering the amplitude of the signals, animals switch from public long-distance communication to private, and sometimes even secret, short-distance communication which is unlikely to be intercepted by those with hostile intentions. Low-amplitude signals are observed in almost all animals which use sound to communicate, notably insects, fish, amphibians, birds and mammals. These signals are used in the contexts of locating sexual partners, maintaining group cohesion and raising the alarm in case of danger. In all cases such signals limit the listening circle to a single individual or to a small number of listeners at close proximity. The reason behind all this hushed whispering is linked to the risk of predation but also, sometimes, to intrasexual competition where males courting females prefer not to be heard and usurped by jealous rivals.[5] Individuals who whisper in this way are indulging in silent flirtation.

Certain moths produce very intense ultrasounds exclusively intended for the attention of females. These sound signals are in a sense the equivalent of birds' territorial songs which rely on sound in order to operate over long distances. However, it has been observed that certain species also produce ultrasounds at a very short distance when their future partners are less than 2 centimetres away. These ultrasounds are emitted by males in response to the release of pheromones, chemical sexual signals, given off by females. The ultrasonic clicking sounds of the males are emitted at a very low volume, dropping as low as 43 decibels measured at 1 centimetre, whereas the ultrasounds emitted in the context of a sexual call or in the combat against bats can be as high as 120 decibels. By reducing their sounds to a murmur, male moths adopt a discreet form of communication which is barely perceptible to other males or to their eternal enemies, the bats with their highly sensitive ears.[6]

The croaking gourami (*Trichopsis vittata*) is a little fish from Southeast Asia often found on sale in pet shops. Gouramis are croakers as they produce a sort of intense grunting or chirping sound during agonistic encounters between territorial individuals, regardless of their gender. During the spawning period, the male and female meet in a nest made of bubbles built underneath a floating leaf. The female makes rippling movements with her body in a vertical position beating her pectoral fins rapidly while the male swims in the traditional horizontal manner. The female then produces a low-intensity sound, a behavioural characteristic which is unique to fish, a sort of purring sound, which is only half as intense as territorial croaking. Like moths, this purring sound is a courtship signal destined exclusively for the attendant male: it allows the release of the gametes to be synchronized – eggs for the female, sperm for the male – and these combine as they float up to the nest of bubbles under its leafy roof.[7] Male and female alike exercise a certain discretion which enables them to avoid being disturbed by other males or spotted by predators.

In the case of another fish, the American silver perch (*Bairdiella chrysoura*), found along the east coasts of the United States, it has been possible to conduct direct tests on the effect of predators on sound communication in males. Silver perch males croak together during the spawning period, forming loud underwater choruses. The principal predator of this fish is the common bottlenose dolphin (*Tursiops truncatus*), a species in which social interactions rely heavily on the exchange of frequency-modulated whistles. Evidence has shown, however, that the chorus of male perches drops by 9 decibels when dolphins are passing in real conditions or when dolphin whistles are artificially broadcast over underwater loudspeakers. The fish do not adopt a state of complete silence but significantly reduce their sound signature as soon as they hear their predators.[8]

The control of vocal intensity in the presence of a predator appears to be rarer in primates. The cotton-top tamarin (*Saguinus oedipus*) is a small monkey native to the humid forests of Colombia. The species, which is extremely sociable and displays highly adaptable behaviour, communicates with the aid of an extensive repertoire of cries which are used during feeding, for group cohesion, moving around, exploration, keeping watch over the immediate environment and raising an alarm. A predator, such as a cat, a marten or a raptor, generally triggers violent intimidatory behaviour. Individuals group together to mob the predator by rushing towards him, their fur bristling, tails erect, accompanying their movements with a torrent of intense cries. In captivity, man – often in the form of supervisory staff members who sometimes need to capture individual animals to administer medical treatment – is also considered a predator and should therefore provoke the same aggressive behaviour. Astonishingly, in experiments conducted at Central Park Zoo in New York, the presence of a supervisor associated with medical treatment did not trigger such reactions. The cotton-top tamarins instead produced whispered vocalizations, barely audible to the human ear. These observations point to the existence of another strategy, perhaps a rare one, in the face of danger – a strategy which is in total contrast to the previous one and in which the intense visual and acoustic demonstrations are replaced by a form of acoustic discretion, in other words, by silence.[9]

Faced with predators, animals, including man, generally display three possible reactions: fight, flight or freeze. Freezing is accompanied with a drop in heart rate due to the action of the autonomous parasympathetic nervous system. This behavioural and physiological state, a form of fear, not only enables the individual concerned to hide but also allows them to be aware of any immediate danger.[10] The complete cessation of any vocal activity is a form of acoustic freezing observed in a great many animal species.

The Túngara frog (*Engystomops pustulosus*) is something of a star amongst amphibians and has been studied from every possible angle with an entire book dedicated solely to its sexual habits.[11] Closely resembling a toad and floating on the surface of the water, males sing in chorus by inflating a large vocal sac. The greatest threat hanging over them is the frog-eating bat or fringe-lipped bat (*Trachops cirrhosis*), a bat with a turned-up nose shaped like the leaf of a tree. This bat hunts down the Túngara frog using all its senses – hearing, sight and echolocation. It is a formidable predator targeting in particular male Túngara frogs which produce the complex vocalizations particularly seductive to females. The dilemma of whether to appeal to the females or remain silent so as not to be gobbled up is an all-consuming one in this case. Observations and experiments with model bats flying over the water have demonstrated a very rapid reaction on the part of the male frogs. In less than a second, the males fall silent and the chorus is interrupted. They freeze and wait for the danger to pass in silence. The frogs only resume their calls after about three minutes.[12] The bats are therefore, without any doubt, a trigger for the frogs' silence.

A long way from warm tropical ponds, in the McMurdo Sound, on the same line of longitude as New Zealand, similar dramas are played out between mammals. Weddell seals (*Leptonychotes weddellii*) gather in summer colonies, from October to December. Settled on near-shore fast ice along the Antarctic coast, the seals care for their young and, when they dive, defend their sexual territories with a very wide variety of sounds, ranging from short, sharp pulses to long and continuous glissades covering a range of frequencies. From mid-December onwards, the vocal activity of Weddell seals drops dramatically by a factor of ten. What is going on? Is this drop simply associated with the end of the reproductive period? It would appear not – this reduction in sound production, a form of individual and collective entry into silence, is largely the consequence of a double danger. In mid-December the ice sheet opens up both naturally, as a result of a rise in temperatures, and artificially with the arrival of ice-breakers. Taking advantage of the new channels and passageways created as a result of this melting ice, two super-predators of the southern waters arrive on the scene – leopard seals (*Hydrurga leptonyx*), another species of seal with impressive jaws, and orcas (*Orcinus orca*), the famous powerful killer whales. Their arrival, marked acoustically by their own vocalizations, coincides with the Weddell seals abruptly falling silent.[13] The silence of the prey coincides therefore with the untimely arrival of a predator.

Still in the Southern Ocean, in the French Kerguelen Islands, marine birds also draw up battle lines. The blue petrel (*Halobaena caerulea*) is a small species of petrel which lives in colonies. Individual birds are vocally active at night when they defend their territories and seduce each other from burrows dug into the dry soil under its cover of island vegetation. Their main predator is another marine bird, the brown skua (*Catharacta antartica*). This bird is a like a wolf for the blue petrels. If recordings of the cries of blue petrels are played to brown skuas – in other words, the cries of the prey to its predator – a clear response to these vocalizations can be observed. In the depths of the night, brown skuas therefore use an acoustic channel to locate their dinner. What happens if, conversely, the cries of brown skuas are broadcast, in other words those of the blue petrels' principal predator? Fight, flight or freeze? The blue petrels stop their vocal activity and adopt a survival silence.[14]

Survival silence does not only exist in birds in far-off places. In more temperate lands, birds of prey, both diurnal and nocturnal, are significant predators of other bird species. Their presence can impose silence on their prey in a similar manner, as has been observed in the dunlin (*Calidris alpina*)[15] and the veery (*Catharus fuscescens*).[16] The fear of others can induce silence across all latitudes, from north to south.

Survival silence can be observed even amongst the biggest and the strongest. As Dian Fossey observed, gorillas stop all activity and fall silent when they sense the approach of humans, the true super-predators whose prey is everything and everywhere.[17]

Achroia grisella is a small nocturnal moth barely 1 centimetre long. Belonging to the Pyralidae family, this cosmopolitan insect would be completely unknown if its larvae did not live in the combs of honey bees (*Apis mellifera*). The larvae are responsible for a considerable amount of damage since they feed on wax and on pollen, boring through the galleries in the combs, leaving webs of silk and transmitting certain diseases to the bees. These bad habits have earned it the vernacular name of the lesser wax moth. Reproduction in adults, who stop eating and survive for no more than one week, takes place outside the hive. Perched on a solid surface, such as the roof of the hive, males produce rapid ultrasonic signals by distorting tiny tymbals situated at the base of the wings. The resulting clicking sounds, each lasting around 100 microseconds at frequencies ranging from 70 to 130 kilohertz, attract females within a radius of 1 to 2 metres distance. The risk of getting swallowed by a bat such as, for example, the greater horseshoe bat (*Rhinolophus ferrumequinum*) is high. When they are not courting and are in flight, the moths dive to the ground as soon as they hear a bat passing. The moths therefore choose flight as a response to danger. But when individuals are about to experience the most crucial moment in their short adult lives, they are in a stationary position and can no longer drop to the ground! Freezing in silence so as not to make the task easier for the long-eared predator appears therefore to be an adapted solution. This is effectively what happens: when a simple ultrasonic clicking sound mimicking a bat is broadcast, both sexes become motionless and the male immediately ceases his sound courtship. The bat imposes a form of *coitus interruptus* no doubt extremely disagreeable for the moths. If this first clicking sound is followed by others emitted at a relatively slow rhythm comparable to that of the bat's sonar during its gleaning activities, the male remains silent for a longer period of time, ranging from a few hundred milliseconds to a minute.[18] This survival silence is therefore of limited duration.ABANDONING silence means facing risks once again. Observation shows that those males which produce the most attractive sexual signals, in other words those with a higher pulse pair rate and peak amplitudes, abandon their silence more quickly than is the case for males generally less likely to be chosen by females, or, in other words, those producing slower and less audible sexual signals. This risk-taking behaviour in the handsome males could in itself be a factor in their selection given that females might prefer the males who remain silent for shorter periods.[19]

Grasshoppers are insects whose sound production is particularly familiar to us. Their loud stridulations, high-pitched and buzzing, invade our summer nights, even in the city. The sword-bearing conehead (*Neoconocephalus ensiger*) is a species of grasshopper common in southeast Canada and northeast United States. They have a green body and the shape of their wings is reminiscent of a blade of grass. Consequently, they are very difficult to see during the day and impossible to see at night. They only betray their presence by their loud stridulations, which act as a sound beacon for numerous predators, notably the northern long-eared bat (*Myotis septentrionalis*). Like the lesser wax moth, the North American grasshopper immediately ceases all sound activity as soon as it becomes aware of ultrasonic pulses reminiscent of the echolocation calls of the northern long-eared bat.[20] This prostration is only possible if the sound pulse of the bat falls between two stridulation patterns of the insect, in other words, during the periods of silence between stridulations. But, in these grasshoppers, stridulation, similar to that of our large green grasshopper, the great green bush cricket (*Tettigonia Viridissima*), is a long series of regularly repeated patterns, like the crumpling of paper or metal. Each pattern lasts approximately 30 milliseconds, followed by a slightly longer silence of about 40 milliseconds, and covers a broad frequency spectrum ranging from around 8 kilohertz up to over 40 kilohertz. These deliberate little silences are effectively listening windows which enable the insects to follow what is going on around them. The survival silence observed in *Neoconocephalus ensiger* is highly effective since experiments conducted with northern long-eared bats show that the bats interrupt their attacks when the grasshopper falls silent.[21] Listening to the enemy relies on a complex neuronal circuit, but one neuron in particular appears to be crucial in the acoustic detection of predators. This is a nerve cell called interneuron T, the name reflecting the shape it forms in the thorax. This cell produces action potentials, those infinitesimal electrical currents which transmit the nerve message, the rhythms of which follow those of the bat's ultrasonic signals.[22] The defence system may therefore seem simple and efficient: a tympan which vibrates, neurons which fire by copying the enemy's sounds and a response which acts as a life-saving reflex. The reality is of course more complex than that. Experience and individual history, the immediate environment such as the presence of members of the same species or of enemies other than the bats, meteorological conditions, vegetation and a great number of other factors, both internal and external, mean that any decisions taken are not simply automatic reactions. The bats are also capable of capturing motionless and silent prey thanks to their echolocation systems. The females of certain grasshoppers, which are mute by nature, are sometimes captured in far greater numbers simply because they are present in greater numbers in certain environments which are less complex than those occupied by the males.[23] Silence is not therefore always effective and being quiet does not offer protection from everything.

A more drastic solution in order to avoid audiophile predators is to move outside their auditory range and simply emit sounds which predators cannot pick up. This means finding an acoustic channel not accessible to the killers and penetrating their physiological silence where no signals can get through. Certain grasshoppers stop using the sounds and ultrasounds targeted by the bats and instead resort to vibrations transmitted by plants. This can be observed in a number of species which stop stridulation but begin to tremulate when bats fly past in the tropical night skies of Panama.[24] By so doing they avoid being detected by their predator.

Ultrasonic signals are not the prerogative of insects and bats. Certain mammals establish a private communication by similarly operating in a domain unoccupied by their predators. Richardson's ground squirrel (*Urocitellus richardsonii*) scampers about on the ground of the vast North American prairies on each side of the border between the United States and Canada. This squirrel has to defend itself against many predators, some of which are sensitive to ultrasonic signals, such as the red fox (*Vulpes vulpes*), coyotes (*Canis latrans*) and domestic cats (*Felis catus*), and others which are incapable of detecting high frequencies, like humans and birds of prey. When a predator is sighted, Richardson's squirrels are known to produce alarm calls which are perfectly audible at a frequency of around 8 kilohertz. These whistling sounds serve as an alarm call to conspecifics, which quickly hide in the burrows they have dug in the soil of the grassy plains. Richardson's squirrels also produce ultrasonic calls, in the form of alarm signals of 48 kilohertz, which for many years went unnoticed since they were totally inaudible to any observers. These alarm calls provoke the same reactions as the ones measuring 8 kilohertz but are clearly undetectable by humans and birds.[25] This strategy of penetrating the physiological silence of others, also adopted by small and large southern and northern flying squirrels (*Glaucomys volcans* and *Glaucomys sabrinus*), two species of North American flying squirrels which glide from tree to tree by stretching open the wide membrane between their front and back limbs and which also converse using ultrasonic calls,[26] ensures them a means of communicating reserved to their dear ones, including the babies huddled between the paws of their anxious parents.

Finally, the last avenue of flight open to prey, when the threat of predators becomes really oppressive, is to abandon sound communication altogether and adopt a permanent state of mutism. A case of losing your voice when someone is eavesdropping a little too closely for comfort. This option, a form of acoustic defeat, has been observed once again in insects, though this time without the intervention of any bats. The American fly (*Ormia ochracea*) is a formidable acoustic hunter. This fly is equipped with a pair of tympans located in the thorax, just behind the head. Two millimetres wide, this ear with its unique mechanism allows pregnant females to locate a sound source with remarkable accuracy in the absence of any visual possibility. They use their ears to track down male crickets and deposit their first-stage larvae on their bodies or immediately alongside them. These larvae, demonstrating a marked absence of good manners, enter the body of the unfortunate cricket without even knocking and this then becomes their larder. From this point on, they live inside the cricket, going through the successive moulting stages and, at their leisure, feeding on the muscles and fatty substances made available to them, albeit unwittingly. After a week, the larva, now much stronger, emerges from the cricket, which, not surprisingly, dies as a result of this exogenous birth process. The larva then transforms into a pupa and, around twelve days later, into a winged adult. The *Ormia ochracea* therefore represents a terrible threat to stridulating crickets. On Kauai Island, in Hawaii, where this fly was inadvertently introduced, oceanic crickets have found a radical solution in that more than 90 per cent of them have quite simply lost the ability to stridulate. This state of total mutism, brought about by what was probably a very simple genetic mutation, makes the stridulatory apparatus in the wings inoperable. The crickets continue to rub their wings but no sound is produced, rather like in those nightmares where we shout for help but no sound comes out of our gaping mouths. The crickets call silently. This morphological tendency appeared over the course of twenty short generations, or over just a few years, and uniquely in response to the threat represented by the parasitoid flies since the crickets from other Hawaiian islands where the flies are less rampant have kept their wings intact and continue to stridulate tranquilly once the sun has gone down.[27] But how do the crickets, which have not disappeared from the island, manage to continue their lovemaking under the coconut trees? Survival silence as a result of morphological mutation seems to be compensated by an increased mobility in males, who cover greater distances in order to find females, while the females, for their part, seem to have developed a tolerance to the absence of sounds, thereby saving local populations.[28]

In this way, resorting to various different techniques, prey succeed in remaining hidden in survival silence. Fragile and threatened, they listen to the movements and sounds of their predators but they are also attentive to the silence which surrounds them. The silence of others is comforting since it indicates the absence of any predator lying in ambush. Any interruption of this silence in the form of so much as a simple movement of air is immediately worrying since it reveals the arrival of danger in some form and puts the whole body on alert, with muscles and senses taut and ready to react at any moment. It is in the interests of predators to shroud themselves in silence if they wish to satisfy their hunger. Yet we know less about the persecutors than about the persecuted. Perhaps this comes from a certain propensity to side with the victim rather than with the executioner.

The survival silence of predators prior to the death of their prey seems an obvious strategy. Close observers of our pets, we immediately think of the inaudible movements of our cats, major killers in our yards and gardens. Lions (*Panthera leo*) are bigger and stronger, but just as silent. They too hunt silently until the moment of attack when their whole body is engaged and the entire savannah is shaken into life. Recordings made directly on the lions' backs, thanks to collars equipped with microphones, clearly show the silence of the hunt before the noise of the attack and the sounds of distress coming from the prey.[29]

What applies to lions is undoubtedly true for almost all cats and probably for many other mammals which use certain auditory capacities to hunt for prey.

For airborne predators, it is all about being able to fly without being noticed, to beat your wings without being heard. Bats' flight is apparently extremely discreet, but it would appear that no naturalist has so far demonstrated interest in the stealthy acoustics of their aerial arabesques. Conversely, the silent flight of owls, major nocturnal predators, has inspired a considerable body of research at the interface between biology and engineering. Seeing an owl fly past in the dark is an unsettling sensory experience. This huge, majestic bird glides like a pale shape in the darkness without leaving any sound trace. The observer is bemused. His eyes tell him that an animal has passed by, yet his ears have registered nothing. The silent flight of these birds is due to the structural properties of their wings – their size and shape and the design and microstructures of the feathers all contribute to a reduction in aerodynamic and rubbing noises.[30] This survival silence, which is not found in diurnal birds of prey, enables owls to reduce their sound impact in the vicinity of their prey and to enhance their own auditory capacities by reducing any surrounding noise. They gain twice over: they are heard less and hear better.

Bats are insatiable insectivores which, as we have seen, provoke survival silences in their prey. In return, for their own benefit, their hunting must be as silent as possible or there is the risk they will fail to get enough food. Most bats which hunt insects on the wing produce very intense echolocation signals. This high intensity has the advantage of ensuring an increased prey detection distance but the disadvantage of perhaps too rapidly alerting prey, in particular moths. The western barbastelle (*Barbastella barbastellus*) is a bat most often found flying around forest edges. This species has opted for an original acoustic solution – it sends out echolocation signals which are from ten to one hundred times lower in amplitude than those of other species. This acoustic discretion, similar to whispering, allows it to get very close to its victims without being detected. This very rare and, on the scale of the evolutionary history of bats, relatively recent strategy seems to give a certain advantage to this species in comparison with other species with more conspicuous echolocation systems.[31]

The North American spotted bat (*Euderma maculatum*) has a different strategy and produces echolocation signals in usually low frequencies, switching from ultrasounds to sounds with low and medium frequencies barely detectable to the moths' ears.[32] Entering into the physiological silence of the prey in this way allows the bat to approach stealthily to a distance of just 1 metre of the future meal. Better to get as close as possible to your plate in order to ensure a decent meal.

Animals therefore engage in deadly trench warfare where survival silence plays a fundamental role. Prey and predators are the nodes of vast and complex trophic networks. Eaters and eaten are linked by the threads of their flight and fight behaviours, and fear, of which survival silence is one expression, is ever present. At the top, man is the hyper-predator of the planet, inducing fear at every level, notably by the sounds and noises he generates. Simply broadcasting recordings of human voices immediately causes pumas (*Puma concolor*) to flee, driving them further afield in the long term and reducing their feeding time.[33] The fear which comes from the top cascades downwards so that the fear of one rapidly becomes the fear of others. Fear is therefore not simply a matter between two enemies but affects a whole ensemble of actors belonging to an ecological system.[34] In the same way, survival silence can be transmitted right through an entire ecological system in such a way that instead of being a simple behavioural response between two isolated enemies silence becomes the driving force of an entire ecology.

17
Solar days

Sometimes, on winter nights, in my unhappy city-dweller's dreams, I am sitting in a Provençal meadow and listening to the cicadas singing their hearts out in the long grass. I remain perfectly still and, for hours on end, observe my favourite animal, the tomenteuse cicada (*Tibicina tomentosa*). This medium-sized insect, scarcely more than 2 centimetres long, is a rare specimen of French fauna, only found in a few grasslands in the Languedoc and the Var, in areas hemmed in on all sides by the threat of construction activity. The tomenteuse cicada stands out because of its distinctive livery – predominantly yellow, picked-out in black and overlain with a shimmering silvery down. Its song is a delicate crackling sound which can last for periods of up to tens of minutes at a time, sometimes interrupted by bursts of somewhat clumsy flight. Everything about this species seems soft – its body, its movements and its sound. It lacks only the affectionate gaze of a young Labrador to make you want to stroke it as you wait for the stars to appear.

The tomenteuse cicada is yellow, and everything around it takes on the same colour – the bleached stones, the clumps of fennel as dry as straw, the sky with its blue bleached out by the blazing sun, the pine trunks on the horizon. Bowing my head under the heat, in the middle of the day, I see this sound, a long acoustic line crossing the plain from one end to another, exactly as I hear it – traced in yellow.

Returning to the little laboratory in Jean-Henri Fabre's Harmas, I transform the day's recordings into images thanks to the Fourier transform, a mathematical operation devised at the beginning of the nineteenth century by the extraordinary Joseph Fourier. Beyond the flickering waves of old-fashioned oscilloscopes, whose grey buttons I used to touch somewhat randomly on the benches of the workshops, the Fourier transform makes it possible to create a sound image, a sonogram, in which three of the fundamental components of sound can be read – time on the horizontal axis, frequencies on the vertical axis and amplitude according to a colour gradient. Seeing sound makes it easier to understand it, especially for those who, like me, have the great misfortune to have a poor ear for music. With the help of these graphics, I can read the sounds and with just a few quick glances, decipher their structures, rhythms and modulations. And, conversely, when I hear a glissando, I can picture the coloured mark it would trace on the screen. The sonogram is a sound picture which can be adjusted at leisure in terms of texture, size, flat tints and colours. When I visualize on my screen the chirping of this delicate tomenteuse cicada, I automatically select a palette of warm colours, ranging from white to red and, of course, constantly passing through the dominant yellow colour. I construct a long grainy soundtrack made up of sun-drenched variations like the song of this sun-loving cicada.

But where exactly is silence in this little cicada which seems never to stop singing in its monochord voice, the colour of sunshine? Today, as in the past, continuously under threat by the European bee-eaters (*Merops apiaster*), those flamboyant but callous insect-eaters, the males and females of my sweet cicada concentrate on what is most important – feeding on sweet sap and finding their soulmate.

After several days of observation, I realize that, for this insect, silence is romantic, nervous or calculating. The song is indeed sustained but it is not totally continuous. Sometimes the males stop their chirping abruptly, and seem to draw a sound breath of barely a single second. I suppose, for I have not carried out enough experiments to be certain, that these rapid pauses allow the singers to listen to what is going on around them and that the sounds of other males pining for love on neighbouring fennel plants makes them very quickly resume their calling for the attention of any females in the vicinity. These little windows of silence, already observed in other insects, are an opportunity to check out the competition. A chance to listen to others in order to assess where they stand in this crazy sexual race.

For a tomenteuse cicada, getting into close proximity with a partner is no easy matter. Perched just a few centimetres above the ground on the main branch of a clump of fennel and highly visible, the male calls continuously, broadcasting in all directions that he is alive, handsome and available. If another male sings too close to him, he changes tone and switches to a chirping that bristles with rivalry and sounds jerky and angry. If this vengeful signal is not enough, the males sometimes confront each other and come to blows until one or the other gives up and goes away. The resident cicada either keeps his place or relinquishes it to the ill-mannered intruder. If the intruder happens to be a female, it is a very different story and she is welcomed with outstretched wings. Female cicadas do not have tymbals, the sound-producing organs which enable males to sing. They are therefore mute, even if some of them can make a clicking sound with their wings. For a male, a silent partner approaching from some distance away is potentially a future sexual partner. In this case, the individual's silence indicates its gender.

When a silent individual comes into sight, the male changes his repertoire and I hear him switching from his long, continuous chirping to a shorter, rhythmical and modulated chirping which is lower in amplitude. He is switching from a public communication to a private one as though under threat from a predator, perhaps a bee-eater. I see for the first time that the male accompanies his acoustic courtship by beating and clicking his wings, which probably helps the female to find him amidst the tangle of vegetation. The female responds to the male by beating her own wings silently, which – and again I am making a supposition here – diffuses volatile molecules. Usually, by exchanging these acoustic signals which are therefore potentially chemical signals, the male and the female successfully find each other and mating takes place. Today, however, the story seems to be somewhat different. Another individual located closer to the ground is keeping silent just like a female. I can, however, just make out the apex of its abdomen and it is not equipped with the indispensable ovipositor which enables the female to lay her eggs in the vegetation. This is a male who seems to be waiting for *a-little-you-know-what*. I turn my attention back to the courting male when, suddenly, I see the other male appear and, with a quick burst of flight, overtake the hard-working first male and mate with the female without having made the slightest effort whatsoever. Under the cover of silence, the second male was hiding while he plotted an evil trick on his rival. The *little-you-know-what* of the silent male was in reality *a-what-males-think-about-all-the-time*. His behaviour demonstrates just to what point the attraction of another's body can lead to some extraordinary moral behaviour, which, if we allow ourselves to tentatively make comparisons with human seduction techniques, would be highly disreputable. A case of waiting for the other to do the hard work, and then sneaking in front of him at the last minute. A truly loathsome bit of evolutionary behaviour where silence becomes a treacherous and unscrupulous tactic.

18

Romantic

In a couple, silence can be a sign of trust (we can enjoy short spells of silence in each other's company like soothing caresses) or of things going downhill (we no longer have anything to say to each other for we are both falling into the same abyss) or of mistrust (we are watching each other suspiciously from a distance). But what does silence mean in other animal species? What is the significance of silence in a sound courtship like that of my little tomenteuse cicada?

If a human can understand and love the poetry of Paul Verlaine even without pausing for breath[1] –

TheresfruitflowersbranchesandleavesThentheres myheartwhichbeatsonlyforyouDonttearitapartwith thosetwowhitehandsItsmyhumblegifttoyourlovely eyes[2]

– what would be the effect of an animal song without any pauses of silence? Apart from a few exceptions, it would resemble a jumble of difficult-to-distinguish sounds. A sound without the silences which surround it is doomed to disappear as first the ears, and then the brain, lose interest and then simply stop hearing it. Even as early as 1888, Georges Louis Leclerc de Buffon observed in his *Histoire naturelle des animaux* the aesthetic and structural importance of the silences in the song of the common nightingale (*Luscinia megarhynchos*): 'These different phrases are interwoven with silences, such silences as, in any kind of melody, compete so powerfully with the powerful effects: we take delight in the beautiful sounds we have just heard, and which continue to ring in our ears; we delight in them all the more because the pleasure is more intimate, more contemplative and is not troubled by any new sensations. Soon we find ourselves waiting, desiring to hear another piece: we hope that it will be the one we took such pleasure from: if we are mistaken, the beauty of the fragment we hear will not allow us to regret the one which is but deferred, and we preserve our hopes intact for the pieces that will follow.'[3]

Like the nightingale's song, most animal sound performances are punctuated with silences which leave the listener hoping for more. These acoustic pauses which wrap around the notes are somewhat neglected in acoustic analyses which tend to focus more on the sounds than on the spaces between them. Just as in engraving and sculpture, however, it is the hollows which allow us to see the shapes. Sounds and pauses form an inseparable couple, so that listening to one without listening to the other wipes out the organized temporal structures where the order, the duration of the different sounds and the pauses code vital information for reproduction and survival. These pauses for breath, which can be an essential part of sexual encounters, represent a new form of silence – a *romantic silence.*

Studies on the role of the temporal architecture of sexual signals abound and cover all animal groups which use sound to communicate. Just as a specimen in a museum collection is catalogued in detail, whenever a song is described, the duration of the sounds and, sometimes, the silences are carefully noted.

In insects and particularly in crickets and grasshoppers, which tend to be studied more frequently than others, silences are an intrinsic part of romantic codes and indicate gender and species. The length of the silences separating the syllables in the stridulations of male bow-winged grasshoppers (*Chorthippus biguttulus*), an insect very common in mainland France, shows little variation and ranges from 10 to 20 milliseconds. Artificially shortening or lengthening these silences by a few milliseconds causes more confusion to the females than does modifying the length of the stridulations by the same amount. If the silences change, the females can no longer use sound to hear and find the males. They like silences which are neither too long nor too short but just long enough for a brief reflection.[4] This preference amongst the females imposes a certain evolutionary stability on the males, since slowing down or quickening the acoustic cadence would serve little obvious purpose.

Another insect, the *Cicada orni*, chirps with such a familiar rhythm that it is almost synonymous with the anthem of Provence. Acoustic patterns alternate regularly and insistently with silences which are slightly longer than the sounds as the ceaseless hammering of the cicada's chirping resonates through the scorched scrublands and pine forests. In the Iberian Peninsula and in North Africa, the cicada orni lives alongside another species, the *Cicada barbara*, to which it bears a close resemblance. The chirping of the cicada barbara is both very similar and very different to that of the cicada orni. The signal is made up of the same acoustic pulses, which are organized in a very similar manner, but the male cicada barbara sings for almost a minute without any pause. For the cicada orni, the regular beat of the coppersmith's hammer; for the cicada barbara, the continuous thud of the jackhammer. The difference between these two species is therefore essentially a tale of silences, present in the orni, absent in the barbara. Yet acoustic experiments have shown that this silence is important. If a recording of the sound of a cicada barbara is played to a male cicada orni, he shows no interest and does not interpret it as the signal of a competing congener. Nor does he show any interest if the silences of the cicada orni are reduced so much that they disappear altogether.[5] Silence is therefore an essential element in the recognition of conspecifics: it marks the species identity.

These romantic silences are not always so pronounced and certain insects adjust to changes in silences, but the rhythm, which is clearly a combination of both sounds and silences, is almost always crucial. When the cicadas stop singing at the end of the day, the great green bush-crickets (*Tettigonia viridissima*) take up the baton and begin beating out their stridulations. In mountain regions, the green bush-crickets can be accompanied by another species, the upland green bush-cricket (*Tettigonia cantans*), which is very close in phylogenetic terms. The great green bush-crickets and the upland green bush-crickets differ essentially in the rhythm of their stridulations – the great green bush-cricket produces stridulations formed of double pulse patterns, while the stridulations of the upland green bush-cricket consist of single patterns. These temporal particularities suggest a different alternation of sound and of silences which allows females to recognize the species identity of their future partner. Although tolerant of temporal lengthening or contraction in the double patterns, the females of green bush-crickets are more sensitive to variations in silence than they are to variations in sounds and they find their way more easily towards males, who respect the length of silences more than of sounds.[6] Silence therefore is by no means negligible; it provides information.

In birds, the song is a complex blend of notes, syllables and sequences. The song is punctuated by silences which cut and break up the acoustic web woven from the tops of the trees. If any changes are made to these silences, everything breaks down and falls apart and the sound signature specific to each species collapses. Listening to a Eurasian skylark (*Alauda arvensis*), the ear is impressed by the diversity of syllables. A single male defending his territory in a wheat field can produce up to 500 different syllables, while we manage to maintain intelligible conversations with the same number of words. These syllables represent an astonishing acoustic variety since the skylark never seems to repeat itself, stringing together rising and falling frequencies which are never the same over several kilohertz and several minutes. But a more prolonged listening quickly reveals a prosody, like a very regular beat – the skylark seems to pour out its message always with the same cadence, like a horse which never alters its pace. Experiments with modified skylark songs show that tessitura, basic frequency and syntax all play a limited role in the coding of the species signature but that, conversely, tempo and rhythm are critically important so that changing the vocal flow partly wipes out the code.[7] The duration of the silences is therefore, once again, an integral part of the romantic code.

If the skylark is a symbolic bird of agricultural landscapes, the Australian zebra finch (*Taeniopygia guttata*) is often known only to the breeders and scientists who keep them in their laboratories. This pretty Australian passerine, which closely resembles an orange-cheeked finch, has become the object of *ex natura* acoustic experiments. Males and females are capable of very refined discrimination of temporal variations and can detect short silences of scarcely 50 milliseconds. Yet certain neurones of the auditive cortex of Australian zebra finches are fired on hearing the syllables, whereas other neurones function during the silences separating these same syllables. There are therefore specific neuronic processes for analysing and decoding silences. These silences are part of the species signature. They differ notably from the silences observed in the Bengalese finch (*Lonchura striata* var. *domestica*), an odd little laboratory bird produced as a result of cross breeding and artificial selection. Neuronal decoding of silences is therefore a vital element in encountering sexual partners belonging to the same species. This system seems moreover to be innate in that when the young of Australian zebra finches are fostered by Bengal finch parents they do not learn the silences of these alien parents but instead express the silences associated with their own species. It is highly likely that in the genetic heritage of Australian zebra finches there is a gene or group of genes associated with silence.[8]

Birds, insects, amphibians, spiders, fish and mammals all produce silences just as they produce sounds. Romantic silence is a sound production which exists, lives and vibrates, as in this description by Stefan Zweig: 'Now the silence began to vibrate, a string without a note.'[9] The rhythms of all sound calls are made up in part of coding silences. How, for example, can we resist the hypothesis that the silences interspersing the calls of whales in controlled sequences[10] do not form part of the codes used to exchange information between fellow users of the oceans?

But true romantic silences are those which form an integral part of conversations, those which lie in the gaps between what one individual and another are saying, the silences which sometimes unite and sometimes separate. In animals, the romantic encounter is often easier when the two partners express themselves and signal to each other. In such cases males and females take part in duets where temporal organization can be very precise, the song of one neatly interspersed with the silence of the other and vice versa, with a precision on the scale of a millisecond, like the rhythmic acoustic ping-pong games of the South American plain-tailed wren (*Pheugopedius euophrys*).[11] In insects, duets can consist of simple interactions, an acoustic to and fro which is repeated until the two partners locate each other and come into physical contact. The most frequently observed principle is the broadcasting of a courtship signal by the male to which the female responds with a discreet and often very brief signal. In this way a minimalistic dialogue is established which, in the case of a couple of southern sickle bush-crickets, or Mediterranean katydid (*Phaneroptera nana*), could be transcribed like this:

– Where are you, Madam Mediterranean Katydid?
– Here, Monsieur Mediterranean Katydid.

Male stridulations are very simple, short and high-pitched, like the soft scraping of fingernails. The females reply without demonstrating much selectivity and accept very variable stimuli, sometimes very different from those offered by the males. In contrast, the length of the silence separating the question and the response shows little variation. For the Mediterranean katydid, for example, it is around 60 milliseconds. The duration of silence-question-response, short as it is, is significant – it is the code of the sound identity of the species, since if this romantic silence becomes too long or too short, the male makes no further attempts to approach the female.[12]

Australian grasshoppers of the *Caedicia* genus also encounter each other thanks to duets in which the silence between the male and the female is equally distinctive. The story seems therefore to be written with the same pen along the lines of: I call you, you respond, we get together, we embrace. But love stories are not always so straightforward and the battle with other hopefuls can be a harsh one. In *Caedicia*, for example, certain silent males take advantage of the situation and, by listening to the duet, manage to locate the females without being seen or heard. Avoiding the fatigue of a sound call, these satellite males therefore take advantage of the efforts made by others in order to win over the opposite sex. But – for there is always a *but* in biology – male seducers who have been potentially hoodwinked seem to have discovered a strategy to avoid being double-crossed at the last minute. In addition to their classic courtship stridulations, they sometimes add another loud sound pattern which coincides with the female's response. In doing so, they cover the female's response to prevent it being detected by the too distant satellite male and thereby guarantee themselves an exclusive dialogue with her.[13]

Satellite males, like those of the Australian grasshoppers, are individuals who deliberately remain silent in the hope of taking advantage of the sounds made by others. They are sometimes considered as sexual parasites, or cleptoparasites, since they are indeed sex thieves. Such a strategy has a triple advantage – not reciting the poetry but claiming the kiss, not singing themselves hoarse with a risk of being overheard by a predator capable of spoiling everything, and conserving their energy for other essential tasks. The satellite tactic has been observed not only in grasshoppers and cicadas, like my tomenteuse cicada in the Mediterranean hills, but also in crickets and amphibians. But who chooses to becomes a satellite rather than a seducer?

In insects, as in amphibians, it would seem that satellites are essentially males less physically favoured, slightly smaller than the others and, when not cowering in silence, producing sounds which are less intense, less deep and, as a result, less attractive for females. Conversely, it is possible that these males may be more agile and speedier when it comes to catching a female. Satellite behaviours have been most successfully observed in natterjack toads (*Epidalea calamita*), a handsome European amphibian distinguished by a long pale line along its back.[14] The singers, assembled around the edge of the pond and calling proudly, are sometimes shadowed by satellites, crouching discreetly less than one metre away. In the majority of cases, a single satellite accompanies a single singer. The two of them form a somewhat ill-matched pair, with the impassioned suitor on one side and the opportunist on the other. Singers and satellites are not assigned to their sexual strategy for their entire lives but can switch from one to the other, sometimes even in the course of a single night, depending on the rivalry between them and their closest neighbours. If a singer finds himself next to a male who is bigger, more vocal and slightly invasive or even vindictive, he might wait in silence and switch over to the satellite side, while the other gets on with the work of seduction in his place. If you disturb a chorus of natterjack toads and remove a singer, the satellite then becomes a singer. If the opposite manipulation is carried out, in other words if you remove the satellite, then nothing happens and the singer remains the singer. The roles of singer and satellite are therefore the consequence of relationships between dominant and dominated, strong and weak. In reality, the switch of status from singer to satellite and therefore from sound to silence, does not depend simply on the nearest neighbour, a form of immediate cause, but on a whole range of social and environmental factors, such as the duration of the reproduction period, the date females first arrive in the vicinity, the density of competing males, meteorological conditions or the pressure imposed by predation rates.[15]

In any event, being able to switch from one strategy to another maximizes an individual's chances of success with female toads – sometimes singing yourself hoarse and having twice as many chances of meeting a female, sometimes remaining silent but expending less energy and taking less risks in the hope of successfully playing dirty.

In certain crickets, development also seems to exert an influence on the reproduction strategy adopted by the males. In the species *Teleogryllus oceanicus*, previously seen turning mute on certain Hawaiian islands in response to the presence of a parasitoid fly, the males reared in silence demonstrated a stronger propensity to become satellites than did the males reared in the acoustic atmosphere of their species. The older they get, the more they too become silent, perhaps through lack of energy, and end up adopting the satellite position.[16]

In the cricket of the North American prairies, the western trilling cricket (*Gryllus integer*), also a victim of parasitoid flies, and for whom silence can be beneficial, satellite males position themselves just a few centimetres away from singing males.

When population density is low, or, in other words, when there are not many individuals in the prairies, singers dominate in number and reproduce more. Conversely, when the density of population is high, the satellite crickets take precedence both in terms of numbers and in reproductive success. The strategy of silence therefore increases in line with population density.[17] A form of equilibrium is nevertheless established between the two strategies with, in the majority of cases, the percentage of satellites not exceeding 15 per cent of the total population since an alternative strategy, in this case falling silent, proves to be effective only if it is a rare event.

Romantic silence therefore plays a vital role in the formation of a couple: a species identity in the songs, waiting time adjusted in duets, or alternative strategies in order to reproduce without being in a hurry. The couple is considered by certain biologists as the first example of sociality, but what role can silence play in the structure of families and of groups? Silence shared by two is good, but when more than two are involved, is it necessarily better?

19

Together

'Be quiet!' Certain silences are disagreeable because they are a sign of submission to an authority. This is the case of the silence imposed at the resumption of lessons or with parental silences during a family meal. These silences are often experienced as a form of injustice since they are dictated by the strongest who impose their signals on others. In non-human animals, this *disciplinary silence* can be observed in interactions between parents and their young for reasons which seem largely irrefutable since, once again, this is ultimately a matter of survival when faced with danger from a predator. Disciplinary silence is therefore closely linked to survival silence.

Newborn birds are in the habit of demanding nourishment from their parents by dint of hungry cries, their beaks wide open like gaping vessels. This caterwauling attracts the attention not only of the exhausted parents but also of predators, which regard the nests as self-service restaurants. The begging cries of the fledglings are therefore, as we have already observed, under a double evolutionary pressure: eat or die. The white-browed scrubwren (*Sericornis frontalis*) is a little forest bird endemic to the southeast coast of Australia. Adults build their nests on the ground or at a height of just a few metres.

The fledglings live under threat from several predators, notably the collared sparrowhawk (*Accipiter cirrocephalus*), a fearsome diurnal bird of prey, and the pied currawong (*Strepera graculina*), a bird which is as much of an opportunist as our European magpie. The baby scrubwrens utter two different call types. The first is a loud request call covering a broad frequency range and made when the parents are in the process of serving up the meal. The second is a more feeble-sounding call, high-pitched in frequency, which is produced when the parent birds are absent and are away from the nest in quest of the next batch of delicacies. These same parents alert their young with a short and scratchy alarm signal, a *buzz*, when they detect a predator on the ground or perched not far from the nest. Experiments with loudspeakers imitating the buzz of frantic parents have shown that the young reduce their begging calls and completely stop their non-begging calls. This alarm signal sent out by the parents is therefore capable of adjusting and even stopping the vocalizations of their young. 'Silence at table!' urge the frightened parents from a distance, for the benefit of their offspring, comfortably ensconced in the nest, their bibs tightly round their necks.[1] Once the fledglings have eaten well and have grown sufficiently, they are able to leave the nest and launch themselves into space. During their first flights they are once again the target of predators but this time in mid-air. The parents of scrubwrens can however help them once again by warning them with a different alarm call, a trill this time, which indicates the presence of an airborne danger. This trill puts a stop to all the vocalizations of the young now frantically attempting to fly and they immediately fall silent at the parents' command. Conversely, any birds which have remained in the nest and are still not yet capable of leaving home pay no attention to this alarm signal, which does not concern them.[2] The abrupt imposition of silence on young white-browed scrubwrens is therefore by no means absolute. Instead, it is contextual and is directed to just some of their young. Conversations around the table with the young fledglings seem to follow certain rules of good upbringing where silence is regarded as an appropriate response. Much better to listen to your parents rather than take a big risk for the sake of a little scrap of food.

What happens when large numbers of conspecifics, exceeding the strict limits of the family group, get together and form choruses in a pond or a forest, on a beach or in a bay? Are animal choruses, whether composed of mammals, birds, amphibians, insects or fish, organized like conservatoire choirs where each voice has a prescribed place and time? Can we find another form of silence here – a *group silence*?

As at the beginning of any piece of music, the silence must first be broken in order for the chorus to start singing. Who gives the signal to begin? The sound chorus starts at the right time of year when meteorological conditions are suitable. The right level of light, the right hygrometry and the right temperature are all essential for the production of the hormones involved in sound behaviours. In vertebrates, melatonin is a hormone secreted by the pineal gland, which, sensitive to light intensity, is a major element in behavioural rhythms throughout the day/night cycle. Steroid sexual hormones, such as testosterone and oestradiol, are produced by the gonads at the appropriate time of the year and these also regulate sound activity. When all the conditions, both internal and external, are met, an individual then takes the initiative to start singing. This individual initiative, linked to a compelling motivation to reproduce, can be enough to trigger the vocalizations of conspecifics positioned nearby. Through a domino effect, the group leader encourages his neighbours and they, in turn, motivate their own neighbours, and so on. This acoustic coconut shy is a consequence of territoriality since each individual defends his or her sexual territory which is under threat from neighbours. The females, notably in grasshoppers, cicadas and frogs, demonstrate a preference for the males who initiate these cascades of song probably because these males are easier to locate given that, even for just a brief moment, they are alone in the acoustic space. This preference for the one who starts first, known in psychoacoustics by the term 'the precedence effect', triggers a race between the males, all eager to be the first to sing. If one of them strikes up, the others have no choice but to follow.

When the entire chorus is in full voice, the psychoacoustic phenomenon of precedence also explains the sound interactions between individuals.[3] In certain species, for example in the ash cicada (*Cicada orni*), individuals sing in harmony, beating time together: I sing with you. On a first listening, these collective sound rhythms seem perfectly synchronized, but in reality there is almost always a slight time lag between neighbouring individuals, with a leader and a follower, the latter following the leader by just a few microseconds. In other species, as in the western saddle-backed bush cricket (*Ephippiger diurnus*), an elegant cricket with its streamlined thorax which produces a short but powerful stridulation from the top of shrubs and bushes, the singers take turns: I sing, you sing. In the case of cicadas, the follower reacts so quickly that his signal keeps pace almost perfectly with that of the leader. In the case of grasshoppers, each individual sings during the other's silence, resulting in alternating signals. Whether in time or out of time, these rhythms suggest that the individuals concerned listen attentively to the others, paying equal attention to the songs and to the silences that surround them. In order to sing together it is essential to listen to what others are saying, but also to what they are not saying. It is important to know how to read between the lines and decode both signals and silences.

Not being able to get a word in edgeways in a lively conversation is often an extremely frustrating experience. Certain animals find themselves confronted with exactly the same problem when they are in large groups and are part of a chorus. If they want to be heard by females, the males must listen to their immediate environment. Where are the others? What are the others doing? Are they calling or silent? Listening to others is the only way of insinuating yourself into the silence of others, the only guarantee of being able 'to get a word in'.

The little tree-dwelling frogs of the genus *Eleutherodactylus* dominate the night-time soundscapes of Central America and the West Indies. With more than 200 different species, they make themselves heard with their very loud croaking, which can reach more than 90 decibels at a distance of 1 metre. The best-known species is the little Puerto Rican common coqui (*Eleutherodactylus coqui*), which gets its name from the two very distinctive notes of its call, *co* and *qui*. Males form choruses at nightfall and until around one o'clock in the morning. Each individual alternates their *coqui* with the *coqui* of their closest neighbour. Singing in the silence of your neighbour can only be achieved thanks to very attentive listening. This propensity of *Eleutherodactylus coqui* to sing between the songs of others has been demonstrated thanks to experiments during which loudspeakers were used to playback artificial sounds made up of a single frequency band, a little more than 1 kilohertz and corresponding to the dominant frequency of the soundscape. These exogenous sounds cause the frogs to fall silent since they are too competitive and do not allow the males to express themselves and to communicate their sexual messages. The only solution for them is to vocalize once the sounds stop, when there is a window of silence. Other experiments show that the males of the *Eleutherodactylus coqui*, but also of other amphibian species, are indeed capable of inserting their own vocalization immediately after the problematic sounds stop. The males can even manage to squeeze their vocalizations into very short silent intervals which are repeated, and therefore predictable, with a duration of a quarter or even a tenth of a second.[4]

The behavioural reactivity of these frogs is remarkable.

Any silence, even a very brief one, is an expressive space left vacant by the others which can usefully be occupied in order to convey your message clearly. The same applies in the case of the cotton-top tamarin, that little Colombian primate which takes to whispering at the approach of medical staff. In an experiment in which captive individuals were subjected to playback sequences of white noise lasting just a few seconds and interspersed with periods of silence of the same duration, the monkeys were observed to adapt very quickly, placing their vocalizations exactly in the windows of silence, just when the message could be successfully communicated. These inserted vocalizations are moreover shorter and louder than vocalizations produced in normal acoustic conditions.[5] These little monkeys, looking for all the world like 1980s rockers, are capable of getting into the rhythm and finding the right timing in order to make the most of the small amount of silence made available to them.

Listening to silence and making silence are disciplinary strategies devised by the dominated who find themselves obliged to adapt to others. However, certain species display more aggressive strategies which take the form of an acoustic domination imposing silence on others, another manifestation of disciplinary silence. Still in the context of sound choruses, certain individuals can dominate vocally and cause their over-talkative conspecifics to fall silent. The African clawed frog (*Xenopus laevis*) is an odd little frog which is totally aquatic and originates from South Africa. Used in the 1950s for pregnancy tests, it was introduced into a great many laboratories and became a model for animal physiology and embryology. Male African clawed frogs have a repertoire of six types of vocalizations, all made up of a rapid series of strange clicks, very different from the sound normally associated with the croaking of an amphibian. When two males meet, one of them has supremacy over the other. The dominant individual then produces twice as many vocalizations as the dominated one, imposing a form of silence on the other. Similar behaviours based on sound dominance have also been observed in insects which rely on tremulation, that is to say insects which cause plants to vibrate by moving around on them. This is the case of the North American black-faced leafhopper (*Graminella nigrifrons*), a little insect scarcely 4 millimetres long and a vector of maize viruses. The males form choruses in which they alternate their calls. This alternation, which is very probably the outcome of a sexual competition, relies on two main mechanisms. First of all, the males only begin to make the plant vibrate if the others are quiet – there must therefore be a silent phase before they can begin to express themselves. If everything is quiet, the males can begin to signal to each other, launching into a sequence of vibrations made up of three parts, increasing in power. If the signal of another individual perched on the same plant is detected during the first part, the warm-up stage in a sense, then the male stops and becomes silent once again.[6] At such times, the activity of others acts as an acoustic inhibitor and imposes silence.

In all these animal sound ensembles, whether in plants, in the air or in water, silences act as regulating elements which are just as important as the signals which come in between them. Silences and signals form a collective machine which seems to have no reason to stop. How is the concert to be ended? What style will the *finale* take? A dazzling crescendo where all the different voices mingle together? Or an abrupt halt, like a break in a rock song? Or a slow descent where everyone finishes *ad libitum*? How can we resume silence after being engulfed in a deafening uproar? Even if considerable interest is shown in how choruses begin, little is known about how they end. Opening ceremonies attract more interest than closing ones, perhaps because the end of a party often brings with it the slightly bitter taste of the return to the day before, to normality.

Singing is an act which uses a lot of energy – the muscles

are in great demand during the process and require a very high consumption of oxygen. Metabolic expenditure during singing can be up to thirty times above that measured during rest. Choruses can sometimes stop simply as a result of fatigue and the need for physiological recuperation.

In certain cicadas, like the palearctic red cicada (*Tibicina haematodes*), the closing stages of a group call can follow similar but opposite rules to the psychoacoustic precedence effect. Towards the end, it will be more advantageous not to start singing, but to finish singing, so as be alone on stage in the final silence. Each individual therefore seeks to end the chorus by adding a final word, just as in an animated conversation we try to bring the debate to a close so as to end up imposing our idea in the freshly restored silence.[7] Having the last word is an indisputable victory.

We have already seen that the presence of a predator is a major obstacle to sound activity: fear of death renders mute.[8] The passing of a bat, a bird of prey, a scavenger or a human can bring a chorus to a halt. All it takes to experience this is to approach a pond pulsating with elastic croaking sounds without making any particular attempt to be discreet: if you take just one step too many, the vocal sacs slacken and the night is plunged into silence once again. South American Túngara frogs (*Engystomops pustulosus*), previously mentioned, form sound ensembles made up of several hundred individuals. Males are heavily preyed on by chiropterans and immediately stop vocalizations when they detect the approach of a bat. Yet an entire chorus can stop abruptly at the approach of a single bat which, clearly, cannot have been detected by all the individuals present. The males do not send out an alarm signal which could alert the whole group. In reality, it is their silence which informs the others of the presence of a danger. The silence carries information and is coded making it *ipso facto* a signal. The silent information is passed on from neighbour to neighbour, and spreads through the entire population in the same way the song of a group leader is the signal for the entire chorus to start singing.[9]

Whatever form they take, such acoustic ends are temporary, existing only as a line of dots left in the space, short intervals allowing you to hide in the wings or to pause for breath. So strong is the motivation to find a partner that choruses quickly resume. But acoustic interactions, in which silence is not a mere absence, are not limited to members of the same species; they also play a role in relations between different species.

20

Sharing

Finally, everything calms down and the hot, humid atmosphere of dawn eases, worn out after so much effort and tension. The forest pauses for breath and the only sounds are a few lingering metallic whistles from some tardy cicadas, and the call of a bird high in the treetops. It is an unfamiliar call for I am a long way from home, in the tropical forest of the State of Veracruz in Mexico, some 9,000 kilometres from Paris. I arrived a few days earlier from the immense capital city of Mexico, swapping the bustling streets of the city centre for the isolated tracks of the forest of Los Tuxtlas. This is my first experience of the tropical world and I have been sent out here on my own to study Mexican cicadas as part of my PhD, though without any very precise goal since, rather like in the good old days, the emphasis seems to be more on simply gaining some experience of the tropics. My first timid steps in the *selva*, on the previous day, might have gone rather better had I not first been greeted by a snake dropping onto my shoulders like a welcoming garland. It turned out to be a vine snake (*Oxybelis aeneus*), handsome and harmless certainly, but a snake nevertheless. Following that, I found myself face to face with a stranger, machete in hand, who greeted me somewhat sternly, as a fellow human certainly, but nevertheless a human. And yet the forest is an enchanting cavern of greenery, a hiding place for marvellous and easy to observe animals including snakes, of course, but also monkeys, birds, spiders, molluscs, butterflies, ants, beetles, dragonflies and blue mosquitoes with their tell-tale red bites!

Every morning at the same time and for the same duration, the identical performance starts up again, at 6.25 am, no sooner, no later, lasting for twenty minutes, never much less and never much more. A few minutes earlier, it is still night and everything is quiet with the forest and humans all asleep, but there is nevertheless the sense that the darkness is in its final moments, something in the air is changing, probably the first rays of the sun, far away but already shining a faint yellow glow in the darkness. Then everything wakes up and the forest seems to stretch before bursting abruptly into life. At that moment an immense animal clamour begins in which the songs of birds mingle with the chirping of cicadas and, sometimes, the howling of monkeys. The air is shaken, torn apart and lifted up by this mass of sound which explodes like a storm. The shrill sound of cicadas fills the ears – seven different species sing together, some with rumbling sounds reminiscent of a railway engine starting up or, rather, like the screech of brakes when an ancient railcar comes into a station. Sounds come from all directions, from below, close to the ground, and from high above, close to the sky. It is an extravagant declaration made by the forest, revealing its true nature and marking the start of a new tropical day.

After this wild profusion of calls, a great silence follows, an intake of breath, like a sigh of relief. The silence which follows the morning chorus is a mass silence, a collective silence, a contrasting silence, a silence of an entire forest gasping for breath.

I am here for the cicadas and so I come back, every morning, to listen to their thunderous awakening. By noting the exact time the chorus starts and finishes, by estimating the height of the singers in the different layers of the leafy canopy, by recording and describing the chirping sounds, I realize that every species evolves in its own individual sound space. I notice in particular a layering of frequencies which makes it possible to share the sound space: each occupies a band of frequencies which barely overlaps that of the others. For example, the species *Quesada gigas*, *Fidicinoides picea* and *Fidicinoides pronoe* follow each other along the frequential scale, the first operating at around 2,200 hertz, the second at around 3,200 hertz and the third at around 4,000 hertz.

After publishing my observations, which I considered very anecdotal, I received an email from a Californian artist who was extremely excited by my story of Central American cicadas.

This stranger was Bernie Krause, whose work represents an international and historical benchmark in soundscape recording. I have to admit that at the time I had no idea who he was. I was unfamiliar with both his artistic work and his scientific contribution to the study of soundscapes.[1] Several years later, on the occasion of an Ecoacoustic congress I was organizing with a mutual friend, Almo Farina, from the University of Urbino in Italy, I invited Bernie Krause to Paris. The first time we met, I took Bernie and his wife Katherine to sip a glass of scalding mint tea in the Grand Mosque of Paris, probably a rather off-beat location for visiting Californians. We talked about soundscapes, acoustic niches, recordings, the artists and scientists who shared our joint passion, and I felt deeply moved to find myself in the presence of such a high-profile musician, equally at home on the violin, the guitar and the Moog synthesizer, collaborator with Pete Seeger, Jim Morrison, George Harrison, Brian Eno, David Byrne, Peter Gabriel, Mick Jagger and Mike Bloomfield, whose blues on a Les Paul I greatly admire.[2] And yet this glorious musical past no longer seemed to hold much interest for him; in a discussion that always remained calm, his voice composed and discreet, it was clear that his attention was now entirely focused on nature and how to protect it. On that day I recognized in Bernie's attitude the same patience, consideration and kindness that I had previously observed in Fernand Deroussen and many other audio-naturalists. It is as though listening to nature, a process which requires patience, isolation, tranquillity and humility, fosters the same calm and calming personalities.

Nevertheless, life has not always been kind to Bernie and Katherine since they were themselves victims of the horrendous Californian wildfires which were the inevitable consequence of climate change.[3] On 9 October 2017, at 2.30 in the morning, their house, Glenn Ellen, situated to the north of San Francisco, was surrounded by flames and they were forced to flee in a state of panic, abandoning their 'wild sanctuary'[4] and leaving behind them an entire life's worth of passion and love. Memories, instruments, writings, much-loved pets were all wiped out by the fury of the flames. Even if copies of Bernie's sound recordings were backed-up in a number of secure places, notably in the collections of the Cartier Foundation in Paris, nothing remained of their life at Glenn Ellen. In the face of such desolation anyone else would surely have been totally devastated. Yet Bernie and Katherine are still there, resilient, enthusiastic, active, still defending and sharing their love for the sounds of nature. Bernie never fails to respond to artistic and scientific requests, lending sounds, sharing his experience, organizing exhibitions and participating in seminars and conferences. During another Ecoacoustic conference some years later, a participant asked him where he found his eternal optimism. Bernie replied, 'I am not sure I am optimistic, I am hopeful.' It was a strange phrase, a kind of oxymoron. It seems in fact that Bernie does not feel positive himself but believes that some people will succeed in resolving the major ecological issues confronting us and that ecoacoustics will help in this effort by drawing attention to the beauty of nature's sounds.

Sometimes, in France, at the beginning of the afternoon when a siesta beckons, I close my eyes and, once again, I am wandering through Los Tuxtlas as morning arrives. All those sounds and silences, both individual and shared, come surging back to me and I find myself hoping that at this very moment they are still resonating, resistant to the ravages of the Anthropocene, just like Bernie Krause himself.

21

Battles

Discretion is a habit prized by smugglers and attackers. Avoiding being seen, avoiding being heard, so as not to give your presence away. Who has not found themselves performing some necessary indiscretions under cover of silence? Who has not crept through long, dark corridors, careful not to speak or to make any rustling or creaking noises so as to observe without being seen, to listen without being heard, to penetrate forbidden zones in search of much-coveted treasures or even to launch an attack on an enemy? This silence of danger is a *battle silence*.

Embarking on daring raids is not the exclusive preserve of curious humans. Chimpanzees (*Pan troglodytes*) also organize high-risk and sometimes warlike forays which can culminate in violent conflicts, as Jane Goodall was able to demonstrate through her tireless observations of the chimpanzee populations in the Gombe forest of Tanzania.[1] Chimpanzee societies are built around communities of several families which together fiercely defend their territories. It is not uncommon for individuals from one community to venture into the territory of a neighbouring enemy community. Jane Goodall witnessed dramatic attacks involving truly warlike tactics in the course of such incursions into enemy territory. The invaders take numerous precautions and are on full alert, listening to the forest, attentive to the slightest sound and, most importantly, avoiding any communication between themselves. Under the cover of the trees, the chimpanzees advance, shrouded in a haze of silence. This self-imposed silence is a weapon of war, a commando strategy, a means of entering enemy territory stealthily and without using force. They need to disappear from the soundscape in order to avoid detection. Suddenly, the encounter with the enemy shatters this circumstantial silence which abruptly and brutally gives way to the fury of the collective attack. Attackers and attacked begin to howl with anger and panic, beating the tree trunks, bending branches and hurling stones. Everything is thrown into turmoil, bodies clash with each other, blows are exchanged and injuries inflicted, branches snap, leaves swirl around, earth is thrown up into the air and the sun disappears in a cloud of rage. There is nothing playful about such encounters, which are genuine battles between clans. They can lead to dramatic scenes involving murder, infanticide and even cannibalism. In chimpanzees, fighting, the second cause of mortality in these primates, begins with a silence and ends in a storm of sound.

As Sabrina Kreif observed in Sebitoli in Uganda, chimpanzees organize other forays which are less aggressive but equally dangerous. Once the sun has set, they leave the protective shelter of the forest and set off under the stars, silently entering fields cultivated by men.[2] Once there, they proceed to do their shopping without paying. Clutching handfuls of stalks or ears of corn, they have learned to control themselves and silence their emotions by suppressing the cries of joy that usually accompany such a haul. These nocturnal expeditions are certainly less warlike, but success still depends on discretion since, if the thieves are heard, they risk being violently pursued and even killed by farmers or their dogs. Silence therefore takes on a vital importance since silent individuals have a greater chance of surviving. All these group silences, motivated by somewhat unsavoury reasons usually associated with battles or looting, are by no means the prerogative of chimpanzees. Other primates are also capable of similar behaviour. The black-handed spider monkeys (*Ateles geoffroyi*) of Central America form societies structured along the same principles as those of chimpanzees, and communities close to the borders often find themselves in conflict. Males set off on raids lasting several hours into unknown territories, exceptionally travelling on the ground in single file and in total silence. Stealthy shadows, the males are on the lookout for available females to capture, sometimes ending up killing their rivals in the process.[3] Silence is once again a prerequisite of success in this sexual quest.

Lions (*Panthera leo*) follow different life rules to chimpanzees and spider monkeys, but the fights between males in order to seduce females do not differ fundamentally. Groups of lions are made up of a dozen females with their young and a few resident males. Certain males live on their own or in small groups, leading a nomadic lifestyle – they do not belong to any clan and go about their business on the margins of groups already formed. The roaring of male lions consists of a deep, low and guttural sound, which carries far across the great grasslands and thorny shrubs of the African savannah. It is a symbol of strength and omnipotence. Playback through a loud speaker of the roaring of a nomadic lion to a resident lion is an interesting bioacoustic experiment, though potentially dangerous for the researcher. These caliphs with their magnificent manes do not appreciate being threatened by pretenders who could take over their thrones, and the roaring of a nomad can lead to virulent, even fatal attacks by the resident males. It would therefore seem prudent for a nomad who is not in a strong position to confront a resident to avoid being heard. Acoustic monitoring of lions shows that nomads in fact roar only very infrequently, to the point of being mute. Resident males therefore indirectly impose a form of silence on nomad males.[4]

Silence is part of battles sometimes waged between members of the same species, but it is also to be found at the heart of interspecies fighting, between individuals belonging to different species. The singing mice of Central America share the mountains of Costa Rica and Panama according to altitude, with the Alston's singing mice (*Scotinomys teguina*) occupying the lower slopes of the mountains while the Chiriquí singing mice (*Scotinomys xerampelinus*) live in the higher regions. Sitting up on their back legs like angry little bears, their necks stretched up, their eyes turned skywards, mouths wide open revealing their tiny teeth, these astonishing little mice seem to be addressing the heavens by singing a series of vocalizations which are loud, varied, complex, rapid and shrill and sometimes ultrasonic. The two species can encounter each other at medium altitudes, between 2,200 and 2,900 metres, on the boundary between their respective zones. On such occasions, what do they have to say to each other? Playback experiments using loudspeakers show that the Alston's brown mice are subordinate to the vocalizations made by the Chiriquí brown mice. The Alston's mice fall silent while the Chiriquí have their say. Conversely, the Chiriquí continue to sing when they hear the Alston's. In the context of sound competition, the relations between the two sister species sharing the same mountain are therefore totally asymmetric, with one imposing silence on the other but the reverse not being true. This unilateral acoustic inhibition is probably a factor in the geographic isolation between the two species.[5] Silence is therefore part of a high-level evolutionary process.

Far from the humid mountains of Central America, the common nightingale (*Luscinia megarhynchos*) of our European forests often sings in company with a cohort of other birds all of which need to defend their territories and seduce females by means of syllables and notes cast into the skies. The acoustic space of the forests, especially at dawn when all the birds are waking up, is rarely empty. Silence is a precious resource during that period. A playback experiment where the songs of other species, notably the willow warbler (*Phylloscopus trochilus*), the robin (*Erithacus rubecula*) or the woodlark (*Lullula arborea*), were played to nightingales revealed remarkable vocal adaptation with the singer avoiding acoustic overlap by placing his own song in the intervals of silence left by the songs of others.[6] This temporal adjustment demonstrates an extraordinary behavioural plasticity, similar to that previously observed in the little frog *Eleutherodactylus coqui* and in tamarin monkeys. The nightingale succeeds in placing its song in the short windows of silence, not by modifying the length of notes but by adjusting the durations of the pauses between its songs. The nightingale, probably in company with other birds, is therefore an animal with flexible acoustic behaviour: it knows how to listen to others and can detect the end of their songs and the intervals of silence which follow them. In less than a second, nightingales react and launch into their own song, instantly filling the available silence. This behavioural flexibility is remarkable since it implies a familiarity with the songs of other species and suggests that these birds, and probably a good many other animal species, do not confine their listening to their fellow species but are also sensitive to the songs of others and even, more broadly, to the soundscapes in which they live. They know how to occupy vacant silences.

Acoustic interactions involving silence are not limited to closely related species, but also concern species from very different zoological groups. Cicadas are capable of producing intense and prolonged sounds which sometimes dominate and even saturate soundscapes. Their chirping can therefore put considerable constraint on other animal species if their songs happen to occupy similar frequency bands. This is what appears to occur in various species of birds and in a species of poisonous frogs from Central America, *Oophaga pumilio*. The cicadas of the tropical forest, notably the very beautiful species *Zammara smaragdina*, with their bodies marbled with jet black and azure blue and their wings highlighted with dark patches, impose their crackly calls on the entire forest and prevent others from expressing themselves, leaving them locked in silence.[7] In this case too, one species imposes its oppressive signal on the other until it becomes impossible for the latter to make itself heard.

Species, whether vegetable or animal, very often find themselves competing for access to certain resources which enable them to live or to ensure their offspring can live and grow – water, organic matter, gases and even light. Competition for a food or energy resource seems inevitable given that hunger and respiration appear to be essential functions for life. Nevertheless, competition also exists over other less obvious resources. These include sound and silence, both of which, as we have seen, are very important both for the survival of individuals and for the continuation of the species. Over the course of evolution, each species finds itself having to use the limiting resource according to a principle which is unique to that species and in such a way that direct competition is avoided. Opting to use a channel which is not used by others is often a good solution in that it is better to remain somewhat isolated by keeping your distance than end up fighting and wasting energy by constantly being in dispute over the same spot. The coexistence of species through avoidance tactics was formalized with the concept of the ecological niche during the first part of the twentieth century. According to George Evelyn Hutchinson from Yale University in the United States, the ecological niche is a multidimensional space of ecological variations, both biotic and abiotic, which are necessary for viability, to say nothing of the Darwinian survival of the species.[8] Each species occupies a niche which is particular to that species and the coexistence of several species at the same place and in the same time appears to be possible if, and only if, the niches of each species do not overlap across the full range of variables. Ecological niche and competition for access to resources are closely linked – by occupying different niches, different species share resources and are therefore no longer in direct competition. The ecological niche is a much-debated concept with its champions and its opponents, but it remains deeply anchored in current Darwinian ecology.[9]

While he was recording soundscapes in the national reserve of Musai Mara in southwestern Kenya, Bernie Krause first sensed that the sound components of the African savannah followed a form of organization, not dissimilar to a symphony orchestra. Each species represented an instrument within a structured whole. Back in the laboratory, visualizing his recordings with the help of sonograms which allowed him to rapidly identify the frequential and temporal characteristics of the sounds, Krause was able to confirm his initial impression. Amphibians and insects, but also elephants and hyenas, seemed to occupy a sound space which was exclusively theirs and, most importantly, one which did not overlap that of others, or only to a negligible extent. Elephants came at the bottom of the scale, with low frequencies, insects were at the top with high frequencies, and amphibians and birds came in between the two. Krause found the same sound structures in other natural sites like the Pic Paradis in Saint-Martin in the French West Indies or in the tropical forest of Borneo in Asia.[10] These observations led him to formulate the niche hypothesis according to which each species occupies an acoustic space, or niche, which belongs exclusively to them and does not overlap that of any other species. Even if he did not specifically refer to Hutchinson's ecological niche theory, the hypothesis of the acoustic niche can clearly be seen as a particular case within Hutchinson's concept. Krause's acoustic niche is an example of an ecological niche defined by a number of acoustic variations.

Impossible to test experimentally, the theory of the acoustic niche is essentially tested by listening to and visualizing the sounds present in a soundscape. If the theory is true, we could expect to see a partitioning of the sound space where the distribution of sounds is made according to species. If it is false, the sounds of each species should appear to be randomly distributed or, on the contrary, with a concentration of sounds in the same zone of the sound space. The theory is tested therefore by analysing sound, the matter, but finally, when everything is taken into account, the theory refers to the sharing of a limited resource, of an unusual resource which is not sound but rather the absence of sound. It is silence that the various species are sharing, silence they seek in order to be able to position their communication signals without the risk of interference from others. It is the silence of silent niches which is precious; silence which drives the evolution of acoustic signals emitted by species cohabiting in the same forest or the same ocean depth. The acoustic niche theory is in fact a theory of shared silence.

Bernie Krause's idea has inspired a great deal of research on amphibians, insects (including the cicadas I was able to observe in Mexico), birds and fish. Results are sometimes contradictory, with some supporting and others contradicting the notion of partitioning, and therefore the existence of acoustic niches, just as happened, in a sense, with the empirical research testing Hutchinson's concept of the ecological niche. In any event, any suggestion that the individuals representing the different species intentionally and rapidly adapt the characteristics of their vocalizations in order to occupy any available silent spaces should be immediately rejected. The behavioural reactions we have seen in nightingales, placing their signals in little windows of silence, are examples of behavioural plasticity where the individuals sending out their signals adjust their behaviour to reflect the immediate environmental context. The acoustic niche hypothesis does not mean that individuals adapt their behaviour in order to occupy the silence. Acoustic niches, if they genuinely exist, will have been modelled by the phenomena of competition at the very slow pace of the evolution of animal species. Any acoustic partitioning we can discern today is the result of slow evolutionary processes.

Competition which develops between species, whether direct or indirect, slow-moving or immediate, represents a series of battles over access to silence. Individuals, motivated by hunger or the need to reproduce, end up fighting in order to make themselves heard, by appropriating the silence for their own use or by imposing silence on others.

These behaviours highlight a unique feature of silence. While it is always possible to continue adding sound to existing sounds, *ad infinitum*, silence is, in itself, confined within strict limits and cannot be either reduced or increased. Silence is a rare and precious commodity. Singers seek out silence in order to express themselves and therefore to break it. Silence is cherished precisely because it can be broken.

22

Where?

The geese we see flying overhead seem to be following fixed and unchangeable migration routes. They fly without ever a backwards glance, going straight to their destination, like bees and ants which, once they have located some food source to share, head directly back to rejoin their companions in their colonies. Animal trajectories raise a great many questions about the methods used by small and large travellers to find their route. We know today that animals possess biological compasses or construct mental spatial maps on both large and small scales, ranging from long transcontinental migratory routes to short journeys flying to and from the nest. Animals are able to establish their location by using information coming from variations in the earth's magnetic field, the polarization of the sun's light, the position of the stars, wave direction, changing levels of salinity, drifting smells, topography and elements of the landscapes along their route.[1] But what about sounds? Do animals also use sound clues to help them find their way? Can sounds coming from landscapes be used as navigational tools? What would happen if these landscapes fell silent?

The importance of sound for moving around seems self-evident for visually impaired people who, as Denis Diderot observed as early as 1749, demonstrate more highly developed auditory capacities.[2] Thanks to a clever trick of cerebral plasticity, paying closer attention to sounds compensates for the absence of visual stimuli. These abilities lead, for example, to the development of a more accurate auditory memory, the capacity to distinguish and identify voices and intonations more precisely and an increased precision in locating sound sources.[3] For the visually impaired, soundscapes are rich in sound clues or, to use Raymond Murray Schafer's terminology, soundmarks, allowing them to work out exactly where they are. During a radio programme, I remember commenting somewhat too hastily that the loud screeching and creaking sound of the Parisian metro was a source of noise since it did not bring any information to city-dwellers. But a visually impaired listener quite rightly pointed out that the sounds of the city, and notably those of the overground metro, are not noises but signals, carrying detailed information about the immediate or more distant environment and the position and speed of objects.

In a more in-depth manner, the Australian John Hull, who became blind at a relatively late stage, aged forty-five, uses his journal to share what it feels like to live without sight. On a number of occasions, he describes soundscapes, generally urban or peri-urban ones, with a precision that demonstrates the remarkable capacities for auditory analysis which appeared after he became blind. Each element of the landscape is presented in such detail that is easy to imagine them both visually and acoustically. Moreover, Hull's sound narratives reveal just how little sound descriptions feature in literature. How many of us can recall learning how to write an auditory description in school even though literacy lessons frequently included exercises based on visual descriptions?

Hull himself writes passionately about certain soundscapes in which animal or plant sounds play a highly significant role. 'In front of me was the lake. It was full of wild fowl. The ducks were quacking, the geese honking, and other birds, which I could not identify, were calling and cranking. There was continual flapping of wings, splashing and squabbling, as birds took off and landed on the surface, or fought over scraps of bread. [...] The trees behind me were murmuring, the shrubs and bushes along the sides of the path rustled, leaves and scraps of paper were blown along the path. I leant back and drank it all in. It was a panorama of movement, music and information. It was absorbing and fascinating.'[4] The description is highly effective – we 'see' the landscape with its stretch of water, its procession of hungry ducks and its rim of lakeside trees. Wind and rain, major sources of geophony, also fascinate Hull, who manages to determine their strength and direction by the sounds they make on his face or on the vegetation or objects around him: 'The blind person experiences the impact of the wind upon his body and the sound of it in the trees.'[5] Earlier in the book, he describes how, for a blind person, the sound of the wind in the trees 'creates trees'.[6] On the subject of rain, Hull observes: 'Rain has a way of bringing out the contours of everything; it throws a coloured blanket over previously invisible things: instead of an intermittent and thus fragmented world, the steadily falling rain creates continuity of acoustic experience.'[7] The attention paid to sound constructs invisible landscapes: 'The more intensely I listened, the more I found I could discriminate, building block upon block of sound, noticing regularities and irregularities, filling dimension upon dimension.'[8] The cessation of external sounds is a threat since it heralds a silence of inexistence. When life stops and movement ceases, when there is no movement and no sound, silence imposes itself and the exterior disappears: 'The world of being, the silent, still world where things simply are, that does not exist.'[9]

Probably less skilfully and far less often than John Hull, we also orientate ourselves using our ears, notably when we cross streets and main roads by listening out for traffic, a method which is becoming dangerous with the new silence of electric vehicles. Main road networks, along with railway lines, church bells or muezzins in villages, are all potentially sound clues which can guide us when, finding ourselves a little lost on a mountain or in a forest, we are anxious to return to civilization. In the era of constant geolocalization, this information from soundscapes may seem redundant, and yet, if we find ourselves momentarily disorientated in the tropical forest because of a recalcitrant GPS, one of our first instincts in order to get our bearings is to listen out for the roar of a river, the pulsating sound of a frog pond or the drone of an engine passing on the nearest track.

Do non-human animals use sounds to find their way in their natural habitats? The use of sounds for long-distance navigation, within or beyond any frontier, remains hypothetical, even if certain observations seem to indicate that pigeons (*Columba livia*) and seabirds may use the infrasounds emitted by the breaking of waves on ocean coasts or by microseisms.[10]

Recent observations tend to show that several animal species use the sounds coming from landscapes to find their way over short or medium distances, in most cases in order to locate or relocate a site associated with reproduction or feeding. We know for example that certain amphibians are attracted by the croaking of congeners who have already found a reproduction site, such as a pond.[11] More astonishing is the attraction of some species for the songs of other species, a phenomenon which lies outside the classic pattern of intraspecies communication.[12] Species do not live in closed acoustic spaces but know how to listen to what lies outside their immediate field. So, for example, the sounds of a pond, a sometimes chaotic mixture of croaking sounds emanating from family members or strangers, can act as an acoustic beacon for individuals still searching for a suitable place for their lovemaking. The same applies to numerous other marine animal species.

Oceans are populated with the tiny mobile larvae of crustaceans, molluscs, cnidarians and fish, all on the look-out for a suitable place to settle, and sometimes attach themselves, where they can feed and reproduce. The seas are large, rocks and coral reefs are small. It is important therefore to know exactly where to go.

Eggs fertilized by fish from coral reefs are carried out to sea by oceanic currents. Far from the shore, the eggs transform into larvae which grow in the open sea and have a mode of life known as planktonic, allowing themselves to be carried freely by the tides and currents. Later in their life cycle, moving from a larval stage to a juvenile stage, the young acquire a certain independence of movement which enables them to move intentionally through the water. The juveniles must then make their way to a site where they can find food, hide from predators and, when they have finally become adults, reproduce. Experiments carried out on the Australian Great Barrier Reef showed that fish larvae were more attracted to acoustically rich sites with a wide range of fish and crustacean sounds than to silent sites. Fish larvae belonging to more than ten different families make their way to reefs by listening to the sounds which emanate from them. Given that sound carries over very great distances in water, these sounds can be picked up from a considerable distance even when the reefs themselves are not visible. Reef sounds, like the sounds coming from ponds, act as sound beacons indicating the location of a place suitable for settlement and reproduction.[13] Astonishingly, these sounds which help fish find their way also attract coral larvae. These are strange creatures which similarly go through two major stages in the course of their ocean-dwelling lives. The adults, or polyps, live in colonies and construct a shared exoskeleton of calcium carbonate which is fixed onto the ocean floor. On a night of a full moon, these sessile individuals release millions of gametes which come together and give birth to planktonic larvae, called planulae. Like fish larvae, these minuscule animals can be carried along by ocean currents before eventually finding a place to anchor themselves. Here too, the sounds of coral reefs seem to play a vital role in orientation. Indeed, experiments have shown that broadcasting the sounds of coral soundscapes over loudspeakers attracts planulae.[14] The larvae of fish and corals seem to follow similar sound pathways and the same is true for the larvae of certain crabs[15] and molluscs.[16]

Coral reefs, one of the richest and most complex ecosystems, are therefore constructed partly by sound. Their richness and their acoustic intensity seem to be in direct correlation to the diversity they shelter. Corals of high environmental quality can attract drifting larvae at greater distances and therefore recruit even more diversity.[17] What will be the consequence if these marine sounds get drowned out by the engine noise of boats transporting useless merchandise or, alternatively, if these same sounds were to disappear altogether as a result of a decline in the quality of reef habitats caused by climate change? Noise, which insinuates itself everywhere like a mudslide, could lead to the loss of sound beacons used as navigational aids for oceanic larvae. Disorientated, these minuscule animals would no longer know in which direction to swim or where to drop their anchor. Experiments carried out in the Moorea Lagoon show very clearly that the noise of motor boats disrupts orientation in coral planulae and that protected marine zones, with less acoustic pollution, attract more larvae than unprotected zones.[18]

The rise in water temperatures has a direct influence on corals, which lose the symbiotic microalgae from which they derive their extraordinary colours. Without these plant allies, the corals become bleached and any surrounding life – anemones, fish, crustaceans, echinoderms, molluscs – begins to decline. This leads to a form of silence which can herald imminent death. Various experimental trials have been devised in the hope of encouraging fish to return. The idea behind these experiments is to address the pelagic larvae of fish, molluscs or coral through loudspeakers, telling them loudly and clearly that this is where they need to begin recolonizing the ailing reef.[19] These acoustic sticking plasters are effective but appear nevertheless limited given the immense scale of the erosion problem affecting vast areas of coral reef.

It is clear that the sounds of landscapes can sometimes function as road signs positioned along the highway to help individuals find their way and locate essential resources. If these are silenced, either because they have disappeared or as a consequence of the presence of human noises, the result can rapidly lead to major disruption on both small and large spatial scales, which can prove fatal. In the light of all this, therefore, what about the silences of the great natural spaces?

23

Great silences

The two of us are looking for cicadas in the scorching Portuguese sun. We are in the countryside not far from Lisbon, exploring olive groves, grasslands, moorland, pine forests and scrubland. We are eager to see all of them, to record all of them, with an unshakable enthusiasm for discovery. We want to experience the particular thrill of first coming across a species previously known only from the descriptions of colleagues, from photographs or scientific publications, of observing for the first time their behaviour and their particular livery with its colours and markings, of knowing for the first time what they look like, what they do, how they are born and how they die. Do they sing in the same way, with the same rhythm, the same intensity, at the same frequencies as those we are familiar with in France? Are they found in the same environments, on the same branches, in the same positions? For us, the chirping of cicadas is an acoustic obsession. Whether driving, walking or simply waiting we are always listening attentively, mapping out the plains and hills with our ears.

Stéphane Puissant, my ever-faithful companion in the field, is an expert in this acoustic quest for cicadas. Always on the alert, whether here in Portugal, in Provence or in Corsica, in

Spain, in Morocco, or even in Senegal or Guinea-Bissau, nothing can get in the way of his determination to become more closely acquainted with these insects, often more easily heard than seen. It was indeed whilst satisfying an urgent need in the mountains of French Cerdanya that he identified, for the first time and using only his ears, a species new to science, the Cerdanya cicadetta (*Cicadetta cerdaniensis*). No matter what the circumstances, he is constantly listening.

We sometimes pause for a little longer, tracking down the soft sounds which might come from discreet little species or, in contrast, the loud uninterrupted crackling of the more garrulous species. Leaving behind an open area full of friendly insects, we step into woodland without really noticing it, our gaze still focused on the ground.

In the space of a single step, everything falls abruptly silent.

We have entered an unexpected silence. Nothing moves, nothing hops or flies, except for a few leaves shaking in the wind. Nothing chirps, or stridulates or sings. Not a single insect can be seen on the tree trunks, not a single bird on the branches. We are in a biodiversity vacuum, a cold and sad silence in a warm and lively country. What is going on? How is this possible? What trap have we stepped into? Finally raising our eyes to gaze above our astonished heads, we realize that the trees around us are neither oaks, nor olives, nor pines, nor pistachios, nor any other Mediterranean species, but tall Australian eucalyptus, ramrod straight. We turn to our Portuguese colleagues who explain that eucalyptus trees are planted in order to mass produce paper pulp for our books, notebooks and newspapers. These fast-growing trees are undoubtedly an economic asset but they are also an indicator of an ecological disaster.

Species from distant origins, born several thousand kilometres away, are rarely appreciated by more local species. Mushrooms, lichens, bacteria, insects and birds have no use for these trunks with their bark hanging in shreds and their white-coated pruinose leaves. Adored by koalas in Australia, eucalyptus trees remain universally unloved in Europe. Planting these trees outside their native zone is a monumental error. Brought far from their native country, they act as a barrier to local diversity and are little more than just packets of lignin pointing skywards, of no attraction for any living creatures. Make no mistake: these trees do not form woods or forests but grow in artificial plantations comparable to those long rows of wheat or maize in the vast cereal-producing plains.

The silence which surrounds these trees uprooted from their native soil is an indicator of a *trompe-l'oeil* version of nature. It is the same silence that we hear in the long lines of poplars planted for the manufacture of cheese boxes, in the rows of fir trees destined to decorate our homes at Christmas, in the straight lines of pines grown for the production of cladding, or in the plantations of rubber trees, their bark sliced open to allow the latex to flow. This silence is an *empty silence*, a silence which is a dramatic indication of ecological imbalance.

In 1962, Rachel Carson published an extraordinarily brave book denouncing with proof and example the devastating and pernicious effects of the widespread use of insecticides and herbicides in agricultural areas of post-war America. This book, now regarded as the birthplace of ecological resistance in the face of the destruction of natural balances and the dire consequences for human health, owes its success to the richness of its far-sighted arguments but also to the choice of an unforgettable title, which is as punchy as the title of a successful musical hit: *Silent Spring*.[1] These two words, short and folksy, were enough to draw attention to a major problem. How can the spring be silent? How can we imagine the return of leaves on the trees, of light and of warmth, without the songs of birds, tree frogs and crickets? Who would not be afraid at the prospect of such a transformation of seasons and landscapes?

The title chosen by Rachel Carson reflects her first chapter, written in the form of a very realistic fable and called 'A fable for tomorrow'. In this chapter an imaginary small North American town finds itself in a near future stripped of all nature and in the grip of a strange and troubling silence. This fable is the starting point for a long investigation which shows how the countryside is being poisoned by chemical products developed to combat insects and plants considered harmful to the food supply and the human economy. The title *Silent Spring* is a reference to the eighth chapter, 'And no bird sings', which could equally be a song title. In this part of her argument, Carson describes the disappearance of large numbers of birds in various towns in the United States after elm trees (*Ulmus* spp.) were treated against Dutch elm disease, a condition which prevents the sap from circulating normally. The spores of the fungus responsible for this infection (*Ophiostoma* spp.) are transported from tree to tree by elm bark beetles (*Scolytus* spp.), insects with dark, stocky bodies which feed on wood. The solution proposed in order to protect elm trees from this fungal attack was to spray DDT, a powerful insecticide used during the Second World War to eradicate typhus and malaria transmitted by fleas and Anopheles mosquitoes. Sprayed abundantly and carelessly onto the elms, the insecticide does indeed locate and kill the elm bark beetles but it also ends up coating the tree's leaves. As happens every autumn, the leaves fall to the ground and are consumed on a large scale by earthworms. The worms end up being eaten by birds, in particular the American robin (*Turdus migratorius*). From creature to creature, the DDT is transmitted through the entire food chain and ends up accumulating in the birds' bodies. The robin population, but also that of dozens of other resident and migratory species, is poisoned, leading to the death or infertility of the individual worm-eaters. The effects on avian populations are so significant that the spring has indeed become silent, emptied of any birdsong.

The situation described by Rachel Carson shows how a form of pollution, chemical in this case, can result in the decline, and even extinction, of animal populations, leading to another, deeply disturbing, example of empty silence.

This is also currently the case for the American pika, or whistling hare (*Ochotona princeps*), a small herbivorous mammal, measuring around twenty centimetres in length and found on the mountain slopes of western North America. Somewhat similar to alpine marmots, pikas whistle loudly at the sight of a predator in order to defend a territory or maintain contact between parents and their young. The vocalizations of pikas are a sound marker of the mountain slopes and often alert hikers to the presence of the species. Protected by their thick fur, pikas have a morphology, a physiology and a biology adapted to cold conditions, to the extent that an extended period of excessive heat, notably during the summer, can prove fatal. Rises in temperature associated with climate change represent an extremely serious problem, and the populations of the Great Basin, east of the Californian mountain range of the Sierra Nevada, are in marked decline. The disappearance of some pika populations leaves a sad gap on the slopes where they once lived. The mountain no longer echoes with the sound of pikas and, here too, the silence is a unmistakeable sign of ecological imbalance.[2]

It was in this same Sierra Nevada that John Muir spent the summer of 1869 and recorded his sense of awe and amazement, inspired by the vast natural landscapes of the American West. In *My First Summer in the Sierra*, as in many other works, the sounds of nature Muir describes are predominantly those associated with rivers and streams, waterfalls, thunder, the wind amongst the leaves.[3] The sounds of animal life feature comparatively rarely – Muir seems to have a stronger inclination to describe vegetable and mineral elements rather than animal ones. Some readers have suggested that the animal silence that emanates from the descriptions of the landscapes he admires might in fact be a reflection of a relative absence of animal life in a natural landscape at that time still ravaged by the pioneers. Wolves, for example, eradicated from this part of the United States, no longer fill the nights with their resonant choruses.[4] The silence of this late nineteenth century, unwittingly transcribed by John Muir, may also be an indication of a crisis in local biodiversity.

In other locations, the uncontrolled arrival of invasive species can trigger a reduction in sound diversity. So, for example, the little fire ant, also known as the electric ant (*Wasmannia auropunctata*), which was introduced into New Caledonia, has had a devastating impact on cricket communities. The fire ants are in competition with the cricket, either indirectly by taking its place in forest ecosystems, or directly, as a predator. In the sites where the ants are rampant, the number of species of crickets and the number of individuals per species have dropped, resulting in an impoverishment of night soundscapes and, therefore, a certain form of silence.[5] Another case, then, where silence can act as a warning for an environmental anomaly.

On a larger scale, in both North America and Europe, the reduction in diversity in bird communities results in a drop in diversity levels in the spring soundscapes of temperate zones, leading to a relative silence which serves as an indication of a global ecological crisis.[6]

Under the seas and oceans, pistol shrimps, those little crustaceans which produce loud snapping sounds with their oversized claws, may one day cease to be heard. Emissions of carbon dioxide (CO_2), the result of human activities, are leading to an increased acidification of the oceans. This chemical imbalance is likely to result in a reduction in sound activity in shrimps which could eventually lead to the disappearance of their acoustic activity, so much a feature of marine soundscapes, and consequently to another alarming silence.[7]

As mentioned previously with reference to the acoustic orientation of pelagic larvae, coral bleaching brings with it a loss of sounds, with the inevitable consequence that any coral reefs affected become markedly more silent.[8]

Even if the use of DDT has been banned since the publication of *Silent Spring*, it is clear that the fable told by Rachel Carson is sadly being re-enacted in a number of other cases and that it could also potentially be rewritten, without too much difficulty, by imagining fields without the buzzing of insects, Provençal hills without the chirping of cicadas, mountains without the whistling of birds of prey or marmots, coastal areas without the cry of gulls, forests without the roar of rutting stags and ocean depths without the grunting sounds of fish.

It is indeed hard not to assume that hundreds of sounds have already disappeared, or will at some point disappear, without even being heard, recorded and documented. Two thirds of coral reefs have already disappeared and 26 million hectares of forest were destroyed between 2010 and 2020.[9] How many sounds were extinguished for ever along with those bleached corals and those fallen trees?

These empty silences, increasingly frequent both on earth and underwater, reveal the impoverishment of biodiversity as a consequence of destruction, exploitation, artificialization, invasion, pollution, climate change and other human attacks. They are the sad indicator of a loss of richness in terms of biodiversity, of a genuine ecological crash.

24

Silence, lockdown!

It is morning but not particularly early.[1] I get up ready for work, and, since it is a lovely day, I open the window above my desk which gives onto the garden. At that point I am struck by a strange sensation, as though it were still night even though the sun has long since risen above the pale line of the horizon. Outside everything seems abnormally quiet. The motorway which slices through the suburbs a few hundred metres away has disappeared and I can no longer hear its constant hum. In the sky, not a single aeroplane from the nearby airports can be seen. The building site opposite remains closed. I cannot hear the sound of hammering.

Suddenly, a sound appears, smooth and crystal clear. It is a blackbird repeating his territorial phrase. He seems to be perched just beside me, on the plum tree which every year produces just a handful of little fruits, enough to put in a Sunday crumble. Then I hear, for the first time, the leaves of the tree stirring in the breeze blowing down from the nearby hills and my eye catches the flight of a bumble bee going from flower to flower in quest of nectar.

I go to the street side to open another window just to make sure. The effect is the same, perhaps even more intense. The town has fallen quiet. There is not a single noise, not a single car going past, no scooters accelerating, no children running to school. It's like a snowy day, when the snowflakes accumulating on the tarmac bring traffic to a halt and absorb all the sounds.

It is March and the weather is dazzlingly beautiful. It will be spring in four days' time and this is the first morning of a strange and serious lockdown.

The abrupt cessation of human activity, decreed in France on 16 March 2020, changed our acoustic environments overnight. With trains idle in stations, planes stationary on the runways, cars left in their garages and pneumatic drills switched off, the noise of human activity came to a halt one bright spring morning and, in its place, came a calm such as had never previously been experienced or even imagined. Suddenly, in city centres in particular, but also in villages, and along the edges of main transport routes, a natural silence reappeared, its potentially soothing effects in stark contrast to the anxiety associated with the suffocating virus.

If life inside our homes was sometimes noisy because of arguments, household appliances, televisions, DIY activities – this was after all the perfect opportunity to do some tiling or drilling – the cessation of human activity had immediate beneficial acoustic effects on life outside.[2] In places where man was not present, noise disappeared. In Paris, Lyon, London, Rome, Milan, Barcelona, Girona, Madrid, Dublin, Stockholm, Kobe, Boston, and in many other towns where acoustic measures were taken, the reduction in sound levels during lockdown was astonishing, measuring in the region of several decibels.[3] In France, the publications of the noise-monitoring organizations Acoucité[4] and Bruitparif[5] reported differences of 3 to 6 dB. These amounts may seem small but, as we have seen, the scale of decibels is deceptive since it is a logarithmic scale and the figure corresponds in reality to drops in the order of 50 to 75 per cent of sound energy. Around the southern runways at Charles de Gaulle airport, the reduction in sound intensity reached a record of 30 decibels, in other words, a historic drop of 99.9 per cent, and those living nearby found themselves in an acoustic environment which was more peaceful than any they had previously known or hoped for.

The impact of the noise of human life on terrestrial life is not only measured in decibels. Questionnaires on the acoustic impact of the lockdown, sent out to several hundred people across the entire world, indicated that the enforced quarantine triggered very positive feelings, in particular associated with calm and quietness.[6] The sound nuisance indicator fell by an average of 61 per cent.

Even if the effects were less significant for people living in areas which were already quiet, such as mountainous regions, this unique experience of a collective acoustic rest demonstrated the omnipresence of sound pollution and opened everyone's ears to the existence of the sounds of nature. 'We discovered birdsong', the cartoonist Plantu observed, in a highly poetic cartoon featuring birds chirruping a series of coloured notes above a white town with wide, spacious streets all completely deserted.[7] We had indeed rediscovered the sounds of nature, which brought colour back into our lives, overshadowed as they were by the dark grey tones of the virus.

We assumed that the birds were singing more than in previous springs. But in the light of what we have already seen of the effect of noise on animals, this hypothesis proved to be incorrect. Since sound pollution had disappeared, the birds were living in healthier conditions and therefore should, on the contrary, have been singing less often and less loudly as there was no need to repeat their messages with increasing intensity. This is exactly what was demonstrated in California with white-crowned sparrows (*Zonotrichia leucophrys*). These birds with their black and white striped skullcaps sang more softly, using broader frequency bandwidths and communicating over greater distances. The reduction in ambient noise, particularly linked to reduced traffic levels, enabled observers to detect singing birds from twice as far away as in normal conditions.[8] It was not that the birds were singing more vehemently, quite the opposite in fact, but simply that Californians could hear them better because the background noise had disappeared. Like them, we became more aware of the songs of blackbirds, tits and robins simply because acoustic conditions were better. Confined to our homes, we were also more available, more willing to devote a little time to observing our immediate environment from our windows. Our locked-down ears, no longer polluted and distracted by uninteresting sounds, were free to discover sounds normally obscured by the noise of machines and of voices.

Birds were not the only ones to benefit from the silence. Under the water, the reduction in marine traffic brought similar benefits for wildlife. In a navigational channel near Pointe-à-Pitre in Guadeloupe, the sound level dropped by 6 decibels during the day.[9] As in the case of birds, the hypothesis might have been that the fish would have taken advantage of this situation to grunt more, but instead the opposite happened. Less disturbed by the vibrations coming from the propellors of passing boats, the fish did not need to repeat their communication signals so often and the number of sounds emitted dropped during the day. We know moreover that a similar drop of 6 decibels occurred in the Atlantic Ocean following the terrorist attacks on New York on 11 September 2001, and that this silence led to a reduction of glucocorticoids measured in the faeces of North Atlantic right whales (*Eubalaena glacialis*), indicating a significant reduction in stress levels.[10] It is therefore highly likely that the whales were able to take advantage of this second human catastrophe and relax during the few weeks of lockdown. Fish and dolphins in the Hauraki Gulf, off Auckland in New Zealand, also benefited from this quiet period and were able to extend their communication range by 65 per cent thanks to a reduction in boat noise amounting to 10 decibels.[11]

The cessation of the anthropophony probably had a great many other positive effects on animal life. Places normally too noisy to be hospitable could be reclaimed and provided new sites for communication and reproduction. Interactions between prey and predators may well have been modified with an increase in the detectability of both.

The return of natural silence, which may have seemed almost insignificant, was in fact highly important for life outside. The acoustic consequences of the lockdown were so significant and on such a global scale that even the earth vibrated less. In normal times, human activity generates high-frequency seismic waves continuously recorded by seismographs, particularly those located in urban environments. During the lockdown, the amplitude of the seismic vibrations in the earth's crust was reduced by 50 per cent to depths of up to several hundred metres.[12]

The cessation of anthropophony meant not only a drop in the overall amplitude of external sounds but, more importantly, a frequential cleansing of soundscapes. Lockdown acted as a filter, cutting out the disagreeable crackling of human activity. The sounds of nature returned, making way for natural silence, and soundscapes became clearer, instantly going from low-fidelity to high-fidelity.

If the silence of gardens, the countryside and other natural spaces was often experienced as a positive event, it is clear that the silence of towns and villages, dominated by asphalt, concrete, stone and glass, could on the contrary be experienced as an oppressive signal, conjuring up the image of life held in suspense and even of death. This perfectly encapsulates the ambivalence of silence – on the one hand an anxious empty silence suggesting the absence of life, on the other a comforting natural silence, rich in animal and plant life.

Human immobility gave the planet a chance to rest, both on land and in the sea, for a period of several weeks – an anthropause, as some have called it – during which animals discovered new and previously unavailable spaces.[13] However, if lockdown seemed interminable to us, for nature it was no more than a short respite, a brief interval. The return of normal human activity rapidly brought with it the return of anthropophony and its toxic effects on natural systems. And natural silence retreated once again.

25

Preserving silence

On the road leading us gently down from the heights of Saint-Pierre-de-Chartreuse to the Dauphine plain – and well before we began to encounter the strange ruins, like industrial ghosts, which serve as a reminder of the exploitation of the mountain by man (a former distillery, a derelict sawmill, abandoned forges) – we rounded a bend and suddenly found ourselves face to face with a mysterious roadside sign, one bearing very little resemblance to the usual canons of the Highway Code.

This large horizontal metal plaque is firmly attached to the forest floor thanks to two grey supports. The writing is by no means recent and the sign has clearly been gnawed by rust, bent under the weight of snow and bleached by rain. In the top right-hand corner, a discreet logo reads 'Office national des forêts'. In the centre, white letters on a pale, almost pastel green background spell out the message: 'Zone de silence du désert de Chartreuse'.

What a surprise! An official zone of silence! Does this mean that, in the midst of this alpine forest, there is really a place where silence is protected? How can that be possible? Why, when and how did the Office national des forêts create such a zone?

A few days later, back in the laboratory again, I began to search online for some explanation as to the origin of this sign, but, much to my surprise, I was unable to find any official internet site which referred to the zone. Nor could I find anything in the pages of ministries, regions, the Office national des forêts, or in the austere columns of the *Journal Officiel*. With nothing to show for my efforts, I used the contact page of the Parc Naturel Régional de la Chartreuse to seek help, though without holding out much hope of getting a reply given that these online forms are often rather like messages in bottles placed in the sea. Nevertheless, the following morning, I was delighted to receive a message from the project manager for the cultural heritage commission who solved the mystery by sending me a copy of the decree issued by the prefecture of the Isère on 8 July 1975. In this text, the subprefect states that 'in view of the importance of retaining within the forest of the Grande Chartreuse zones of calm and silence in the interests of the public good and for the benefit of hikers [. . .] the use of any motorized vehicle (cars, motorcycles, mopeds, etc.) [and] the use of transistors, and any other acoustic instruments such as tape recorders, record players, etc. [are prohibited]'. Attached to this very brief text is a map on a 1:25,000 scale delineating, with the aid of a thick and rather clumsy line, a zone covering a dozen or so square kilometres surrounding the Grande Chartreuse monastery. The zone of silence is indeed a statutory area where noise is prohibited for the benefit of all.

Curious to discover this area which I felt must be unique in France, I went back a few months later on a brief assignment. How wonderful to find myself for the very first time in the Chartreuse mountains during the spring. The national park staff, with whom I had remained in contact, showed me a different world. The white tones of the snow and ice had been replaced by myriad shades of green with new leaves and tender plants.

We entered the zone of silence from the Correrie, a low monastery building which served for a time as the infirmary and has now been transformed into a museum. Taking the track which follows the foot of the Bachais valley, chosen in 1084 by Bruno le Chartreux as the site of his hermitage in view of its isolated position (the monks referred to the area as 'le désert'), we come across another sign, reminding us of the need to be silent. This one looks considerably less official than the one erected by the Office national des forêts and features a stylized gothic arch under which a monk is depicted in profile, wrapped in his cowl, the long hooded robe so closely associated with monastic life.

The sign indicates the true story. The zone of silence is not for the benefit of hikers, nor for that of birds, but for the monks who seek solitude and isolation. The national park staff confirm that the zone of silence in fact came about as the result of a request made by the monks and addressed to the prefecture. After the Second World War, the monastery attracted large numbers of tourists who began to arrive in coaches, cars or on motorbikes. Disturbed by the noise of all this hustle and bustle, the monks succeeded in obtaining this prefectural decree which even today has no equivalent in France. The 'public good' is in reality a 'religious good'.

After a very warm welcome from the lay administrator of the monastery, we made our way past the main buildings with their soaring gothic architecture, and on past the little saw mill run by the monks. Following the Saint-Bruno stream we passed in front of Notre-Dame de Casalibus, a tiny chapel which marks the beginning of the path to the Col de la Ruchère, which we quickly reached. We dropped down a little further to the west through the Habert meadows, carpeted with thick gentians, one of the 130 plants that are used to make the famous green liqueur distilled by the monks.

The landscape of the 'désert' is a well-balanced mix of firs and beeches, of pastureland, steep slopes and unobtrusive and harmonious stone buildings. All is calm and restful, very much conducive to contemplation and reflection. It also transpires, somewhat surprisingly, that the rare noises which can be heard in this privileged environment no longer come from visitors and hikers but from the monks themselves. Even if they live in the silence of their cells and their prayers, the brothers mark the passing of time with the toll of their bells, spend time in the various workshops, run the saw mill and obtain supplies from outside. They live within this zone and, inevitably, generate a thousand and one little noises. This is the very essence of the paradox of noise and silence – we often ask others to be silent without being aware of the noise we make ourselves.

A little further away, outside the zone, we find other signs on the roadsides. These are designed and put in place by a local organization campaigning against vehicle noise, and motorbikes in particular. A Eurasian eagle-owl (*Bubo bubo*), the emblem of the national park, hoots to anyone listening: 'Silent Chartreuse, happy Chartreuse.' The mysterious nocturnal bird, symbol of wisdom, reminds us that silence is indeed a shared asset which should be respected and preserved.

All this signage reminds me that, in the past, the word 'silence' was written under the large white letter 'H' on signs indicating the proximity of a hospital. Passers-by were asked to be silent so as not to disturb the rest of the sick and convalescents. So why not do the same at the entrance to nature reserves by displaying a little symbol which would invite visitors to exercise a certain discretion by respecting the peace of the site and of its inhabitants?

A considerable amount of research has shown the beneficial effects of contact with natural environments. A walk in an urban park, in the countryside, by the sea, in a forest or on a mountain has positive physiological effects which reduce the risk of strokes, high blood pressure, asthma and cardiovascular diseases,[1] while the psychological benefits lead to a reduction in negative emotions such as anger, fatigue or sadness and to an increase in concentration capacities and in feelings of satisfaction and enjoyment.[2] The positive experience of contact with natural elements obviously involves all five senses, but vision and hearing are probably the most stimulated given that a natural landscape is above all enjoyed with our eyes and ears. It seems obvious that a feeling of well-being could be easily triggered by the sight of an open landscape with a clear horizon and a bright sky and without any polluting clouds or oversized human constructions. The same applies when it comes to sounds: a walk or a hike in a peaceful acoustic atmosphere untroubled by noises triggers a feeling of serenity which is beneficial to body and mind.[3] Escaping from a town to explore natural spaces allows people to get away from acoustic stress and to benefit from restful places.

Appreciating a natural silence is cited as the second most important reason why Americans visit natural parks, coming just after the desire for fresh and pure air. These parks are favoured places for hikers because of their natural sounds, in particular those associated with rivers, the wind and birds.[4] A single passing plane, helicopter, car or any other motorized vehicle can undermine feelings of well-being and significantly detract from the value of protected sites.[5] The absence of noise and the presence of birdsong allows people to reach a state of well-being through contact with a natural environment.[6]

It might be hoped that the various regulatory instruments for the protection of nature would indirectly provide protection from noise, but protected zones are not immune to anthropophony. In France, the forest of Risoux in the Haut-Jura is a magnificent site with considerable ecological value, home to a remarkable fauna including the capercaillie, the famous bird, three-toed woodpeckers, wolves and lynx. Protected by various measures for nature conservation,[7] this forest nevertheless still suffers from high levels of acoustic pollution due to the presence of flight paths of planes landing and taking off from Geneva airport. It is estimated that air traffic noise constitutes 75 per cent of the soundscape.[8] This forest therefore represents a splendid natural landscape trapped in a severely degraded acoustic atmosphere in which it is difficult to find natural silence. In national parks, the overflight of recreational aircraft is forbidden below a height of 1,000 metres and drones are prohibited from flying over some nature reserves, undoubtedly limiting one form of noisy intrusion. There are also local initiatives such as the 'zones de nature et de silence' as defined by the Parc Natural Régional du Luberon, which aims to protect the exceptional avifauna including in particular Bonelli's eagle (*Aquila fasciata*) and the Egyptian vulture (*Neophron percnopterus*). Zones of quiet and non-disturbance have been introduced in certain parks and reserves providing access to places less affected by noise.

More generally, American national parks, although relatively silent because of restrictions on human activity, are nevertheless polluted by human noise, particularly when they are located not far from urban zones.[9] In Europe, the European Environment Agency powerfully acknowledged the importance of quiet in its territories by publishing a report mapping out quiet areas. According to this agency, only 18 per cent of non-urban European zones could be considered as quiet and 27 per cent of Europe's Natura 2000 zones as havens of quiet.[10] The five quietest European states are Iceland, Norway, Sweden, Finland and Greece. A natural silence is therefore more likely to be found in these countries outside urban areas. In all countries, the quietest sites are, not surprisingly, sites which are sparsely populated, with few major transport links and generally at high altitudes. Only 5 per cent of continental France and Corsica could potentially be classified as quiet areas, the majority of these being in the Alps, the Pyrenees, the central mountains of Corsica and the humid zones of the Mediterranean coast. The European Environment Agency struggles to force member states to reduce the harmful effects of noise on human health and biodiversity. Almost always close to a road or under a flight path, it is very difficult to identify a genuinely quiet zone in France. Audio-naturalists are only too aware of this, sometimes having to struggle for several hours for a single minute of recording without noise.

Non-institutional actors also tend to sound the alert and to take action. In the United States, the audio-naturalist Gordon Hempton spent a long time searching for a single square inch[11] of the earth's surface where natural silence would reign supreme. This noise fugitive ended up placing a small red stone in the centre of the Hoh rainforest in the Olympic National Park near Seattle in Washington State.[12] This symbolic, even artistic, gesture reveals the hegemony of human noise which leaves only a few square centimetres of quiet. Through this gesture, Hempton seeks also to protect much more than a tiny space: by protecting silence in a single spot, it is possible to protect an entire space – a forest – since sounds and noises occupy large volumes, far greater than that of a single stone.[13] Following in Hempton's footsteps, the international organization Quiet Parks International sets out to identify and grant awards to sites which are especially quiet.[14] In France, the Mountain Wilderness Association runs a Franco-Italian programme, with the unequivocal title 'Silence!', which aims to combat the sounds of quadbikes, motorbikes, all-terrain vehicles, snowmobiles, tourist planes and helicopters which hamper enjoyment of the mountains.[15] For the seas and oceans, however, there do not appear to be any quiet areas which are protected from the noises of navigation or shipyards.

What can be done to combat noise and preserve natural silence? Since ears, unlike eyes, cannot be closed, the first reflex in a quest for silence is above all to protect ourselves, to erect barriers between ourselves and the outside world. We devise acoustic armour in the form of earplugs, noise-cancelling headphones, thick walls, absorbent panels, double-glazed windows. We find solutions using partial insulation, escaping from noise, withdrawing into ourselves. We focus our attention on the silence of our inner spaces and pay little or no attention to external silences, to the silences of other living beings. Reducing noise at its source, in other words as near as possible to the machines which generate it, is rarely prioritized. And yet it is only by diminishing the noises of friction and flow, by reducing the noise of internal combustion engines, by limiting the speed of our journeys, perhaps even by developing a more restrained attitude and restricting our own movements, that we can succeed in reducing our acoustic waste.

In addition, we should reintroduce natural sounds in the way that certain animals such as lynx and bears have been reintroduced. By incorporating native and varied forms of vegetation in artificialized spaces like certain urban, industrial, commercial or agricultural zones, the songs of birds, crickets, grasshoppers and amphibians will be more evenly distributed.

The solution to any societal problem cannot bypass education. It is vitally important to raise awareness across the entire population of the harmful effects of noise and of the need to preserve zones where noise is not welcome. Before pointing a finger, we might instead want to take a close look at our own actions, our own movements. We are often disturbed by others, but are we not ourselves also sources of noise? We have learned, with varying degrees of success, not to throw rubbish out of the window and even to pick up litter, and now it is time to ensure that we stop carelessly allowing noise to spill out around us, time to stop unashamedly polluting the sound spaces we share with other living beings.

Conclusion

Silence is therefore multiple and 'full of secrets', as Vladimir Nabokov suggested.

Silence can be absolute (an impossible form), natural (a restful form), physiological (a deaf form), dead (a form to eliminate), survival (a necessary form), romantic (a heart-shaped form), disciplinary (in the form of a big stick), group (a form of bond), battle-like (a warmongering form) or it can be empty (a form of loss).

Silence exists on every level, on every scale, ranging from a few centimetres to several square kilometres, from a few microseconds to several hours, from an individual level to entire ecosystems. It is internal and external, individual and collective, disturbing and comforting.

Silence is by no means an emptiness, an absence or a negation. It is rich and contains information essential to animal communication and to the structuring of natural systems. It is a contested resource and a space to be filled.

Conclusion

In the cloister of the Abbey of Saint-Martin-du-Canigou in the Pyrenees, monastic silence is depicted on the carved capitals in the form of monks with large ears and small mouths. Without reference to a religious belief but in line with scientific knowledge, perhaps we too should become a little misshapen, reducing the size of our mouths and enlarging our ears in an attempt to restore the sound equilibrium of the world. Listening to silences and sometimes embracing silence also means reflecting a little on our behaviour and our ecology.

Shhh!

Notes

Chapter 2
1. H.C. Gerhardt and F. Huber, *Acoustic Communication in Insects and Anurans*, Chicago: University of Chicago Press, 2002, p. 531.
2. R. Boistel, T. Aubin, P. Cloetens et al., 'How minute sooglossid frogs hear without a middle ear', *Proceedings of the National Academy of Sciences*, no. 110, 2013, pp. 15360–4.
3. H.D. Thoreau, *Journal. Volume 4*, New York: Dover Publications, 1962, p. 90.
4. R.M. Schafer, *The Soundscape: The Tuning of the World*, Rochester, VM: Destiny Books, 1994.
5. E.O. Wilson, *Biophilia: The Human Bond with Other Species*, Cambridge, MA: Harvard University Press, 2009, p. 1.

Chapter 3
1. F.-R. Chateaubriand, *Atala – René – Les Aventures du dernier Abencérage*, Paris: GF-Flammarion, 1998.

Chapter 4
1. B. Krause, *Voices of the Wild: Animal Songs, Human Din, and the Call to Save Natural Soundscapes*, New Haven, CT: Yale University Press, 2015.

2 R. C. Mishra, R. Ghosh and H. Bae, 'Plant acoustics: in search of a sound mechanism for sound signaling in plants', *Journal of Experimental Botany*, no. 67, 2016, pp. 4483–94.
3 P.S. Hill and W. Wessel, 'Biotremology', *Current Biology*, no. 26, 2016, R187–R191.
4 M. Pagnol, *My Father's Glory and My Mother's Castle*, London: Picador, 1991, p. 73.
5 J. Muir, *Nature Writings*, New York: Literary Classics of the United States, 1992.
6 T. Lengagne, T. Aubin, J. Lauga and P. Jouventin, 'How do king penguins (*Aptenodytes patagonicus*) apply the mathematical theory of information to communicate in windy conditions?', *Proceedings of the Royal Society B: Biological Sciences*, no. 266, 1999, pp. 1623–8.

Chapter 6

1 C.E. Shannon and W. Weaver, *The Mathematical Theory of Communication*, Champaign: University of Illinois Press, 1949.
2 According to the terminology created by Michel Boulard in M. Boulard and B. Mondon, *Vies et memoires de cigales*, Barbentane: Equinoxe, 1995.
3 V. Nabokov, *Collected Stories*, London: Penguin, 2010, p. 16.
4 J.C. Dunn, L.B. Halenar, T.G. Davies et al., 'Evolutionary trade-off between vocal tract and testes dimensions in howler monkeys', *Current Biology*, no. 25, 2015, pp. 2839–44.
5 T. Lecocq, S.P. Hicks, K. Van Noten et al., 'Global quieting of high-frequency seismic noise due to COVID-19 pandemic lockdown measures', *Science*, no. 369, 2020, pp. 1338–43.
6 S. Linke, T. Gifford, C. Desjonquères et al., 'Freshwater ecoacoustics as a tool for continuous ecosystem monitoring', *Frontiers in Ecology and the Environment*, no. 16, 2018, pp. 231–8.
7 N. Jones, 'The quest for quieter seas', *Nature*, no. 568, 201, pp. 158–61.
8 C.M. Duarte, L. Chapuis, S.P. Collin et al., 'The soundscape of the Anthropocene ocean', *Science*, no. 371, 2021, eaba4658.

9. H. Slabbekoorn, R.J. Dooling, A.N. Popper and R.R. Fay, *Effects of Anthropogenic Noise on Animals*, New York: Springer, 2018.
10. G.J. Vermeij, 'Sound reasons for silence. Why do molluscs not communicate acoustically?', *Biological Journal of the Linnean Society*, no. 100, 2010, pp. 485–93.
11. M. Troianowski, N. Mondy, A. Dumet, C. Arcanjo and T. Lengagne, 'Effects of traffic noise on tree frog stress levels, immunity and color signalling', *Conservation Biology*, no. 31, 2017, pp. 1132–40.
12. C.D. Francis, N.J. Kleist, C.P. Ortega and A. Cruz, 'Noise pollution alters ecological services: enhanced pollination and disrupted seed dispersal', *Proceedings of the Royal Society B: Biological Sciences*, no. 279, 2012, pp. 2727–35.
13. Ademe, I Care and Consult, Energie Demain et al., 'Estimation du cout social du bruit en France et analyse de mesures d'évitement simultané du bruit et de la pollution de l'air', 2021, https://librairie.aderne.fr.
14. J. Zinsstag, E. Schelling, D. Waltner-Toews and M. Tanner, 'From "one medicine" to "one health" and systemic approaches to health and well-being," *Preventative Veterinary Medicine*, no. 101, 2011, pp. 148–56.
15. Ibid.
16. Slabbekoorn et al., *Effects of Anthropogenic Noise on Animals*.

Chapter 7
1. J.-H. Fabre, *The Life of the Fly*, London: Hodder and Stoughton, 1913, pp. 4–5.

Chapter 8
1. E.A. Poe, *Great Short Works*, New York: Harper Collins, 2004, p. 174.
2. R. Frison-Roche, *First on the Rope*, New York: Prentice Hall, 1950, p. 40.

3. T. Mullet, S. Gage, J. Morton and F. Huettmann, 'Temporal and spatial variation of a winter soundscape in South-Central Alaska', *Landscape Ecology*, no. 31, 2015, pp. 1117–37.
4. S. Dagois-Bohy, S. Ngo, S.C. du Pont and S. Douady, 'Laboratory singing sand avalanches', *Ultrasonics*, no. 50, 2010, pp. 127–32.
5. P. Valery, *Odds and Ends* (*Tel Quel*). This translation from *Collected Works of Paul Valéry. Volume 2: Poems in the Rough*, translated by Hilary Corke. Princeton: Princeton University Press, 1969, p. 166.
6. M. Genevoix, *Ceux de 14*, Paris: Garnier-Flammarion, 2018.
7. J. Alper, 'Antinoise creates the sounds of silence', *Science*, no. 252, 1991, pp. 508–9.
8. J.G. Lilly, 'Designing the quietest room in the world', *Journal of the Acoustical Society of America*, no. 146, 2019, p. 2767.

Chapter 9

1. V. Frapat, *Le Bruit du silence*, compagnie De-ci de-là, 2020, www.compagnie-decidela.fr.
2. F. Deroussen, *Silence des hommes*, double CD, Naturophonia, Chiff-Chaff, 2020.
3. A. Camus, *Notebooks 1935–1942*, New York: Alfred A. Knopf, 1963, p. 206.
4. Ibid., p. 107.
5. J.-J. Rousseau, *Reveries of the Solitary Walker*, Oxford: Oxford University Press, 2011, p. 103.
6. W. Whitman, from 'Song of Myself', in *A Choice of Whitman's Verse*, London: Faber and Faber, 1968, p. 49.
7. A. de Saint-Exupéry, *Wind, Sand and Stars*, London: Heinemann, 1939, p. 93.
8. R.M. Schafer, *The Soundscape: The Tuning of the World*, Rochester, VM: Destiny Books, 1994.

Chapter 11

1. É. Faure, *History of Art: Ancient Art*, New York: Harper & Brothers, 1921, p. 6.

2 P.M. Gray, B. Krause, J. Atema, R. Payne, C. Krumhansl and L. Baptista, 'The music of nature and the nature of music', *Science*, no. 291, 2001, pp. 52–4.
3 R.M. Schafer, *The Soundscape: The Tuning of the World*, Rochester, VM: Destiny Books, 1994, p. 5.
4 P. Schaeffer, *In Search of a Concrete Music*, Berkeley: University of California Press, 2012.
5 Interviews with Antoine Golea, 1957, https://catalogue.bnf.fr/ark:/12148/cb38503106d. This translation found on rcm.ac.uk.
6 F.-B. Mâche, *Music, Myth, and Nature, or The Dolphins of Arion*, Chur: Harwood Academic Press, 1992.
7 D. Rothenberg, *Nightingales in Berlin: Searching for the Perfect Sound*, Chicago: University of Chicago Press, 2019, p. 93.
8 J.D. Rothenberg, *Bug Music: How Insects Gave Us Rhythm and Noise*, London: Picador, 2014.
9 J.R. Cooley and D.C. Marshall, 'Sexual signaling in periodical cicadas, *Magicicada* spp. (Hemiptera: Cicadidae)', *Behaviour*, no. 138, 2001, pp. 827–55.
10 D. Rothenberg and M. Deal, 'A new morphological notation for the music of humpback whales', *Art & Perception*, no. 3, 2015, pp. 347–58.
11 E.L. Dolittle and H. Brumm, 'O canto do uirapuru: consonant pitches and patterns in the song of the musician wren', *Journal of Interdisciplinary Music Studies*, no. 6, 2012, pp. 55–85.
12 E.L. Doolittle, B. Gingras, D.M. Endres and W.T. Fitch, 'Overtone-based pitch selection in hermit thrush song: unexpected convergence with scale construction in human music', *Proceedings of the National Academy of Sciences*, no. 111, 2004, pp. 16616–21.
13 M. Araya-Salas, 'Is birdsong music? Evaluating harmonic intervals in songs of Neotropical songbird', *Animal Behaviour*, no. 84, 2012, pp. 309–13.
14 B. Krause, 'The niche hypothesis', *Soundscape Newsletter*, no. 6, 1993, pp. 6–10.

15 D. Rothenberg, T.C. Roeske, H.U. Voss, M. Naguib and O. Tchernichovski, 'Investigation of musicality in birdsong', *Hearing Research*, no. 308, 2014, pp. 71–83.
16 S. Earp and D. Maney, 'Birdsong: is it music to their ears?', *Frontiers in Evolutionary Neuroscience*, no. 4, 2012, p. 14.
17 https://youtube/3jbHbDena_U?t=2282
18 https://www.dailymotion.com/video/x6eOn3x (at 19'20).

Chapter 12

1 Popul Vuh. PDF version at www.latinamercianstudies.org/maya/Popol_Vuh.pdf.
2 J.L. Brant and J.L. Fozard, 'Age changes in pure-tone hearing thresholds in a longitudinal study of normal human aging', *Journal of the Acoustical Society of America*, no. 88, 1990, pp. 813–20.
3 J. Sueur and S. Puissant, 'Similar look but different song: a new Cicadetta species in the montana complex (Insecta, Hemiptera, Cicadidae)', *Zootaxa*, no. 1442, 2007, pp. 55–68.

Chapter 13

1 C. Mora, D.P. Tittensor, S. Adl, A.G.B. Simpson and B. Worm, 'How many species are there on earth and in the ocean?', *PLOS Biology*, no. 9, 2011, pp. 1–8, and A. Chapman, *Numbers of Living Species in Australia and the World*, Department of the Environment and Heritage, Australia, 2006.
2 K.C. Catania, 'Worm grunting, fiddling and charming: humans unknowingly mimic a predator to harvest bait', *PLOS ONE*, no. 3, 2008, pp. 1–13.
3 P.G. Mota and G.C. Cardoso, 'Song organization and patterns of variation in the serin (*Serinus serinus*)', *Acta Ethologica*, no. 3, 2001, pp. 141–50.
4 K.S. Henry, M.D. Gall, G.M. Bidelman and J.R. Lucas, 'Songbirds trade off auditory frequency resolution and temporal resolution', *Journal of Comparative Physiology A*, no. 197, 2011, pp. 351–9.

5 R. Nakano, T. Takanashi, T. Fujii, N. Skals, A. Surlykke and Y. Ishikawa, 'Moths are not silent, but whisper ultrasonic courtship songs', *Journal of Experimental Biology*, no. 212, pp. 4072–8.
6 T.E. Holy and Z. Guo, 'Ultrasonic songs of male mice', *PLOS Biology*, no. 3, 2005, e386.
7 C. Luo, C. Wei and C. Nansen, 'How do "mute" cicadas produce their calling songs?', *PLOS ONE*, no. 10, 2015, e0118554.
8 Pérez-Granados and K.-L Schuchmann, 'Vocalizations of the greater rhea (Rhea americana): an allegedly silent ratite', *Bioacoustics*, no. 30, 2020, pp. 564–74.
9 J. von Uexküll, *A Foray into the World of Animals and Humans*, Minneapolis: University of Minnesota Press, 2013.
10 W. Feuerhahn, 'Du milieu à L'*Umwelt*: enjeux d'un changement terminologique', *Revue philosophique de la France et de l'étranger*, no. 134, 2009, pp. 419–38.
11 Von Uexküll, *A Foray into the World of Animals and Humans*, p. 87.
12 T. Nagel, 'What is it like to be a bat?', *The Philosophical Review*, no. 83, 1974, pp. 435–50.

Chapter 14
1 J. P. Hume, 'The history of the dodo *Raphus cucullatus* and the penguin of Mauritius', *Historical Biology*, no. 18, 2006, pp. 69–93.
2 D. Quammen, *The Song of the Dodo: Island Biogeography in an Age of Extinctions*, London: Random House, 2012.
3 P. Éluard, *Poésie ininterrompue*, Paris: Gallimard, 1969 (English translation here by Helen Morrison).

Chapter 15
1 P. Senter, 'Voices of the past: a review of Paleozoic and Mesozoic animal sounds', *Historical Biology*, no. 20, 2008, pp. 255–84.
2 C. Gervaise, J. Lossent, C. A. Valentini-Poirier, P. Boissery, C. Noel and L. Di Iorio, 'Three-dimensional mapping of the benthic invertebrates biophony with a compact four hydrophones array', *Applied Acoustics*, no. 148, 2019, pp. 175–93.

3 S.A. Darroch, E.F. Smith, M. Laflamme and D. H. Erwin, 'Ediacaran extinction and Cambrian explosion', *Trends in Ecology & Evolution*, no. 33, 2018, pp. 653–63.
4 C. Radford, A. Jeffs, C. Tindle and J. Montgomery, 'Resonating sea urchin skeletons create coastal choruses', *Marine Ecology Progress Series*, no. 362, 2008, pp. 37–43.
5 M. Solé, M. Lenoir, J. M. Fontuño, M. Durfort, M. van der Schaar and M. André, 'Evidence of Cnidarians sensitivity to sound after exposure to low frequency noise underwater sources', *Scientific Reports*, no. 6, 2016, 37979.
6 J.E. Samson, T.A. Mooney, S.W.S. Gussekloo and R.T. Hanlon, 'A brief review of cephalopod behavioral responses to sound', in A.N. Popper and A. Hawkins, *The Effects of Noise on Aquatic Life II*, New York: Springer, 2016, pp. 969–75.
7 C. Darwin, *The Expression of the Emotions in Man and Animals*, Oxford: Oxford University Press, 1998, p. 89.
8 H. Song, O. Béthoux, S. Shin et al., 'Phylogenomic analysis sheds light on the evolutionary pathways towards acoustic communication in Orthoptera', *Nature Communications*, no. 11, 2020, 4939.
9 D.B. Weishampel, 'Dinosaurian cacophony', *Bioscience*, no. 47, 1997, pp. 150–9.
10 Z. Chen and J.J. Wiens, 'The origins of acoustic communication in vertebrates', *Nature Communications*, no. 11, 2020, 369.

Chapter 16

1 J. Zeng, N. Xiang, L. Jiang et al., 'Moth wing scales slightly increase the absorbance of bat echolocation calls', *PLOS ONE*, no. 6(11), 2011, pp. 1–6.
2 T.R. Neil, Z. Shen, D. Robert, B.W. Drinkwater and M.W. Holderied, 'Thoracic scales of moths as a stealth coating against bat biosonar', *Journal of the Royal Society Interface*, no. 17, 2010, 20190692.
3 B.E. Roche, A.I. Schulte-Hostedde and R.J. Brooks, 'Route choice by deer mice (Peromyscus maniculatus): reducing the

risk of auditory detection by predators', *The American Midland Naturalist*, no. 142, 1999, pp. 194–7.
4   H.R. Goerlitz, S. Greif and B.M. Siemers, 'Cues for acoustic detection of prey: insect rustling sounds and the influence of walking substrate', *Journal of Experimental Biology*, no. 211, 2008, pp. 2799–806.
5   D.G. Reichard and R.C. Anderson, 'Why signal softly? The structure, function and evolutionary significance of low-amplitude signals', *Animal Behaviour*, no. 105, 2015, pp. 253–65.
6   R. Nakano, T. Takanashi, T. Fujii, N. Skals, A. Surlykke and Y. Ishikawa, 'Moths are not silent, but whisper ultrasonic courtship songs', *Journal of Experimental Biology*, no. 212(24), 2009, pp. 4072–8.
7   F. Ladich, 'Females whisper briefly during sex: context- and sex-specific differences in sounds made by croaking gourmis', *Animal Behaviour*, no. 73, 2013, pp. 379–87.
8   J.J. Luczkovich, H.J. Daniel, M. Hutchinson et al., 'Sounds of sex and death in the sea: bottlenose dolphin whistles suppress mating choruses of silver perch', *Bioacoustics*, no. 10, 2000, pp. 323–34.
9   R. Morrison and D. Reiss, 'Whisper-like behaviour in a non-human primate', *Zoo Biology*, no. 32, 2013, pp. 626–31.
10 K. Roelofs, 'Freeze for action: neurobiological mechanism in animal and human freezing', *Philosophical Transactions of the Royal Society B: Biological Sciences*, no. 372, 2017, 20160206.
11 M.J. Ryan, *The Túngara Frog: A Study in Sexual Selection and Communication*, Chicago: University of Chicago Press, 1992.
12 M.D. Tuttle, L.K. Taft and M.J. Ryan, 'Evasive behaviour of a frog in response to bat predation', *Animal Behaviour*, no. 30(2), 1982, pp. 393–7.
13 J.A. Thomas, 'Silence as an anti-predation strategy in Weddell seals', *Antartic Journal*, no. 22, 1987, pp. 232–4.
14 F. Mougeot and V. Bretagnolle, 'Predation risk and moonlight avoidance in nocturnal seabirds', *Journal of Avian Biology*, no. 31, 2000, pp. 376–86.

15 K.N. Mouritsen, 'Predator avoidance in night-feeding dunlins *Calidris alpina*: a matter of concealment', *Ornis Scandinavica (Scandinavian Journal of Ornithology)*, no. 23, 1992, pp. 195–8.

16 K.A. Schmidt and K.L. Belinsky, 'Voices in the dark: predation risk by owls influences dusk singing in a diurnal passerine', *Behavioural Ecology and Sociobiology*, no. 67, 2013, pp. 1837–43.

17 D. Fossey, 'Vocalizations of the mountain gorilla (Gorilla gorilla beringei)', *Animal Behaviour*, no. 20, 1972, pp. 36–53.

18 M.D. Greenfield and M. Baker, 'Bat avoidance in non-aerial insects: the silence response of signaling males in an acoustic moth', *Ethology*, no. 109, 2003, pp. 427–42.

19 N. Cordes, T. Schmoll and K. Reinhold, 'Risk-taking behaviour in the lesser wax moth: disentangling within – and between – individual variation', *Behavioural Ecology and Sociobiology*, no. 67, 2013, pp. 257–64.

20 P.A. Faure and R.R. Hoy, 'The sounds of silence: cessation of singing and song pausing are ultrasound-enduced acoustic startle behaviours in the katydid Neoconocephalus eniger (Orthoptera: Tettigoniidae)', *Journal of Comparative Physiology A*, no. 186, 2000, p. 129–42.

21 H.M. ter Hofstede, J.M. Ratcliffe and J.H. Fullard, 'The effectiveness of katydid (*Neoconocephalus ensiger*) song cessation as antipredator defence against the gleaning bat *Myotis septentrionalis*', *Behavioural Ecology and Sociobiology*, no. 63, 2008, pp. 217–26.

22 P.A. Faure and R.R. Hoy, 'Neuroethology of the katydid T-cell II: responses to acoustic playback of conspecific and predatory signals', *Journal of Experimental Biology*, no. 203, 2000, pp. 3243–54.

23 H. Raghuram, R. Deb, D. Nandi and R. Balakrishnan, 'Silent katydid females are at higher risk of bat predation than acoustically signalling katydid males', *Proceedings of the Royal Society B: Biological Sciences*, no. 282, 2015, 20142319.

24 J. Belwood and G. Morris, 'Bat predation and its influence on calling behavior in Neotropical katydid', *Science*, no. 238, 1987, pp. 64–7.
25 D.R. Wilson and J.F. Hare, 'Animal communication: ground squirrel uses ultrasonic alarms', *Nature*, no. 430, 2004, p. 523.
26 M.N. Murrant, J. Bowman, C.J. Garroway, B. Prinzen, H. Mayberry and P.A. Faure, 'Ultrasonic vocalizations emitted by flying squirrels', *PLOS ONE*, no. 8, 2013, pp. 1–6.
27 M. Zuk, J.T. Rotenberry and R.M. Tinghitella, 'Silent night: adaptive disappearance of a sexual signal in a parasitized population of field crickets', *Biology Letters*, no. 2, 2006, pp. 521–4.
28 S.L. Balenger and M. Zuk, 'Roaming Romeos: male crickets evolving in silence show increased locomotor behaviours', *Animal Behaviour*, no. 101, 2015, pp. 213–19.
29 M. Wijers, P. Trethowan, B. du Preez et al., 'The influence of spatial features and atmospheric conditions on African lion vocal behaviour', *Animal Behaviour*, no. 174, 2021, p. 63–76, and S. Chamaillé-Jammes, personal communication.
30 C.J. Clark, K. LePiane and L. Liu, 'Evolution and ecology of silent flight in owls and other flying vertebrates', *Integrative Organismal Biology*, no. 2, 2020, obaa001.
31 H. Goerlitz, H. Hofstede, M. Zeale, G. Jones and M. Holderied, 'An aerial-hawking bat uses stealth echolocation to counter moth hearing', *Current Biology*, no. 20, 2010, pp. 1568–72.
32 J. Fullard and J. Dawson, 'The echolocation calls of the spotted bat *Euderma maculatum* are relatively inaudible to moths', *Journal of Experimental Biology*, no. 200, 1997, pp. 129–37. Echolocation is not confined to ultrasounds. Certain species of birds use echolocation based on audible signals, see S. Brinkløv, M.B. Fenton and J. Ratcliffe, 'Echolocation in oilbirds and swiftlets', *Frontiers in Physiology*, no. 4, 2013, pp. 123.
33 J.A. Smith, J.P. Suraci, M. Clinchy et al., 'Fear of the human "super predator" reduces feeding time in large carnivores', *Proceedings of the Royal Society B: Biological Sciences*, no. 284, 2017, 20170433.

34 L.Y. Zanette and M. Clinchy, 'Ecology of fear', *Current Biology*, no. 29, 2019, R309–R313.

Chapter 18

1 D.C. Mann, W.T. Fitch, H.-W. Tu and M. Hoeschele, 'Universal principles underlying segmental structures in parrot song and human speech', *Scientific Reports*, no. 11, 2021, p. 776.
2 P. Verlaine, *Selected Poems*, Oxford: Oxford University Press, 1999, p. 89.
3 G.L. Leclerc de Buffon, *Histoire naturelle des animaux*, Paris: Lecène et Oudin, 1888.
4 D. Von Helversen and O. Von Helversen, 'Recognition of sex in the acoustic communication of the grasshopper *Chortippus biggutulus* (Orthoptera, Acrididae)', *Journal of Comparative Physiology A*, no. 180, 1997, pp. 376–86.
5 P.C. Simões and J.A. Quartau, 'Selective responsiveness in males of *Cicada orni* to conspecific and allospecific calling songs (Hemiptera Cicadidae)', *Entomologia Generalis*, no. 29, 2006, pp. 47–60.
6 J. Schul, 'Song recognition by temporal clues in a group of closely related bushcricket species (genus *Tettigonia*)', *Journal of Comparative Physiology A*, no. 183, 1998, pp. 401 10.
7 T. Aubin and J.-C. Brémond, 'The process of species-specific song recognition in the skylark *Alauda arvensis*: an experimental study by means of synthesis', *Zeitschrift für Tierpsychologies*, no. 61, 1983, pp. 141–52.
8 M. Araki, M.M. Bandi and Y. Yazaki-Sugiyama, 'Mind the gap: neural coding of species identity in birdsong prosody', *Science*, no. 354, 2016, pp. 1282–7.
9 S. Sweig, 'Unexpected acquaintance with a craft' (1934). This translation at www.prosperosisle.org/spip.php?article1190=
10 J.N. Schneider and E. Mercado III, 'Characterizing the rhythm and tempo of sound production by singing whales', *Bioacoustics*, no. 28, 2018, pp. 239–56.

11. N.I. Mann, K.A. Dingess and P.J.B. Slater, 'Antiphonal four-part synchronized chorusing in a Neotropical wren', *Biology Letters*, no. 2, 2006, pp. 1–4.
12. E. Tauber, D. Cohen, M.D. Greenfield and M.P. Pener, 'Duet singing and female choice in the bushcricket *Phaneroptera nana*', *Behaviour*, no. 183, 2001, pp. 411–30.
13. T.J. Hammond and W.J. Bailey, 'Eavesdropping and defensive auditory masking in an Australian bushcricket, *Caedicia* (Phaneropterinae: Tettigoniidae: Orthroptera)', *Behaviour*, no. 140, 2003, pp. 79–95.
14. A. Arak, 'Callers and satellites in the natterjack toad: evolutionarily stable decision rules', *Animal Behaviour*, no. 36, 1988, pp. 416–32.
15. J.R. Lucas, R.D. Howard and J.G. Palmer, 'Callers and satellites: chorus behaviour in anurans as a stochastic dynamic game', *Animal Behaviour*, no. 51, 1996, pp. 501–18.
16. N.W. Bailey, B. Gray and M. Zuk, 'Acoustic experience shapes alternative mating tactics and reproductive investment in male field crickets', *Current Biology*, no. 20, 2010, pp. 845–9.
17. G.A. Rowell and W.H. Cade, 'Simulation of alternative male reproductive behavior: calling and satellite behaviour in field crickets', *Ecological Modelling*, no. 65, 1993, pp. 265–80.

Chapter 19

1. D. Platzen and R.D. Magrath, 'Parental alarm calls suppress nesting vocalization', *Proceedings of the Royal Society B: Biological Sciences*, no. 271, 2004, pp. 1271–6.
2. R.D. Magrath, D. Platzen and J. Kondo, 'From nestling calls to fledgling silence: adaptive timing of change in response to aerial alarm calls', *Proceedings of the Royal Society B: Biological Sciences*, no. 273, 2006, pp. 2335–41.
3. M.D. Greenfield, M.K. Tourtellot and W.A. Snedden, 'Precedence effects and the evolution of chorusing', *Proceedings of the Royal Society B: Biological Sciences*, no. 264, 1997, pp. 1355–61.

4 R.D. Zelick and P.M. Narins, 'Intensity discrimination and the precision of call timing in two species of Neotropical treefrogs', *Journal of Comparative Physiology*, no. 153, 1983, pp. 403–12.
5 S.E.R. Egnor, J.G. Wickelgren and M.D. Hauser, 'Tracking silence: adjusting vocal production to avoid acoustic interference', *Journal of Comparative Physiology A*, no. 193, 2007, pp. 477–83.
6 R.E. Hunt and T.L. Morton, 'Regulation of chorusing in the vibrational communication of the leafhopper *Graminella nigrifrons*', *American Zoologist*, no. 41, pp. 1222–8.
7 J. Sueur and T. Aubin, 'Acoustic communication in the Palaearctic red cicada *Tibicina haematodes*: chorus organization, calling-song structure, and signal recognition', *Canadian Journal of Zoology*, no. 80, 2002, pp. 126–36.
8 The French verb used here is *amuïr* – to make mute. The author points out that this is a rarely used verb that it was impossible not to use at least once (Trans.).
9 A.L. Dapper, A.T. Baugh and M.J. Ryan, 'The sounds of silence as an alarm call in túngara frogs, *Physalaemus pustulosus*', *Biotropica*, no. 43, 2011, pp. 380–5.

Chapter 20

1 B. Krause, *The Great Animal Orchestra: Finding the Origins of Music in the World's Wild Places*, Boston and New York: Little, Brown, 2012, and *Voices of the Wild: Animal Songs, Human Din, and the Call to Save Soundscapes*, New Haven, CT: Yale University Press, 2015.
2 M. Bloomfield, A. Kooper, S. Stiller, *Super Session*, Castle Communications, 1973.
3 B. Krause, 'The sound of disappearance', XXII Triennale di Milano, *Broken Nature: Design Takes on Human Survival*, 2018, www.brokennature.org.
4 www.wildsanctuary.com

Chapter 21

1. J. Goodall, *Through a Window: My Thirty Years with the Chimpanzees of Gombe*, Boston: Mariner Books, 2010.
2. S. Krief, *Chimpanzés. Mes frères de la foret*, Arles: Actes Sud, 2019.
3. F. Aureli, C.M. Schaffner, J. Verpooten, K. Slater and G. Ramos-Fernandez, 'Raiding parties of male spider monkeys: insights into human warfare?', *American Journal of Physical Anthropology*, no. 131, 2006, pp. 486–97.
4. J. Grinnell and K. McComb, 'Roaring and social communication in African lions: the limitations imposed by listeners', *Animal Behaviour*, no. 62, 2001, pp. 93–8.
5. B. Pasch, B.M. Bolker and S.M. Phelps, 'Interspecific dominance via vocal interactions mediates altitudinal zonation in Neotropical singing mice', *The American Naturalist*, no. 182, 2013, E161–E173.
6. H. Brumm, 'Signalling through acoustic windows: nightingales avoid interspecific competition by short-term adjustment of song timing', *Journal of Comparative Physiology A: Neuroethology, Sensory, Neural, and Behavioral Physiology*, no. 192, 2006, pp. 1279–85.
7. C.Q. Stanley, M.H. Walter, M.X. Venkatraman and G.S. Wilkinson, 'Insect noise avoidance in the dawn chorus of Neotropical birds', *Animal Behaviour*, no. 112, 2016, pp. 255–65, and W.P. Pàez, B.C. Block and A.S. Rand, 'Inhibition of evoked calling of *Dendrobates pumilio* due to acoustic interference from cicada calling', *Biotropica*, no. 25, 1993, pp. 242–5.
8. G.E. Hutchinson, 'Hommage to Santa Rosalie or why are there so many kinds of animals?', *The American Naturalist*, no. 93, pp. 145–59.
9. A. Pocheville, 'La niche écologique. Histoire et controverses récentes', in T. Heams, P. Huneman, G. Lecointre and M. Silberstein (eds.), *Les Mondes darwiniens. L'évolution de l'évolution*, Paris: Éditions Matériologiques, 2011, pp. 897–933.

10 B. Krause, 'The niche hypothesis', *Soundscape Newsletter*, no. 6, 1993, pp. 6–10.

Chapter 22

1 H. Mouritsen, 'Long-distance navigation and magnetoreception in migratory animals', *Nature*, no. 558, 2018, pp. 50–9.
2 D. Diderot, *A Letter About the Blind for Those Who See*, Stuttgart: Newcomb Livraria Press, 2023.
3 M. Rychtarikova, 'How do blind people perceive sound and soundscape?', *Akustika*, no. 23, 2015, pp. 1–4.
4 J. Hull, *Notes on Blindness: A Journey Through the Dark*, London: Profile Books, 2017, p. 65.
5 Ibid., p. 91.
6 Ibid., p. 4.
7 Ibid, p. 17.
8 Ibid., p. 112.
9 Ibid., p. 66.
10 S.C. Patrick, J.D. Assink, M. Basille et al., 'Infrasound as a cue for seabird navigation', *Frontiers in Ecology and Evolution*, no. 9, 2021, p. 812.
11 V. Buxton, M. Ward and J. Sperry, 'Use of chorus sounds for location of breeding habitat in two species of anuran amphibians', *Behavioral Ecology*, no. 26, 2015, pp. 1111–18.
12 A. Fouquet, T. Tilly, A. Pašukonis et al., 'Simulated chorus attracts conspecific and heterospecific Amazonian explosive breeding frogs', *Biotropica*, no. 53, 2021, pp. 63–73.
13 S.D. Simpson, M. Meekan, J. Montgomery, R. McCauley and A. Jeffs, 'Homeward sound', *Science*, no. 308, 2005, p. 221.
14 M.J.A. Vermeij, K.L. Marhaver, C.M. Huijbers, I. Nagelkerken and S.D. Simpson, 'Coral larvae move toward reef sounds', *PLOS ONE*, no. 5, 2010, e10660.
15 J.A. Stanley, C.A. Radford and A.G. Jeffs, 'Location, location, location: finding a suitable home among the noise', *Proceedings of the Royal Society B: Biological Sciences*, no. 279, 2012, pp. 3622–31.

16 A. Lillis, D.B. Eggleston and D.R. Bohnenstiehl, 'Oyster larvae settle in response to habitat-associated underwater sounds', *PLOS ONE*, no. 8, 2013, pp. 1–10.
17 J.J. Piercy, E. Codling, A. Hill, D. Smith and S. Simpson, 'Habitat quality affects sound production and likely distance of detection on coral reefs', *Marine Ecology Progress Series*, no. 516, 2014, pp. 35–47.
18 D. Lecchini, F. Bertucci, C. Gache et al., 'Boat noise prevents soundscape-based habitat selection by coral planulae', *Scientific Reports*, no. 8, 2018, 9283.
19 B.R. Williams, D. McAfee and S.D. Connell, 'Repairing recruitment processes with sound technology to accelerate habitat restoration', *Ecological Applications*, no. 31, 2021, e02386.

Chapter 23

1 R. Carson, *Silent Spring*, Boston and New York: Houghton Mifflin, 1962.
2 E.A. Beever, 'Ecological silence of the grasslands, forests, wetlands, mountains, and seas', *Conservation Biology*, no. 23, pp. 1320–2.
3 J. Muir, *My First Summer in the Sierra*, Edinburgh: Canongate, 2007.
4 P.A. Coates, 'The strange stillness of the past: toward an environmental history of sound and noise', *Environmental History*, no. 10, 2005, pp. 636–65.
5 A. Gasc, J. Anso, J. Sueur, H. Jourdan and L. Desutter-Grandcolas, 'Cricket calling communities as an indicator of the invasive ant *Wasmannia auropunctata* in an insular biodiversity hotspot', *Biological Invasions*, no. 20, 2018, pp. 1099–111.
6 C.A. Morrison, A. Auniņš, Z. Benkő et al., 'Bird population declines and species turnover are changing the acoustic properties of spring soundscapes', *Nature Communications*, no. 12, 2021, 6217.
7 T. Rossi, S.D. Connell and I. Nagelkerken, 'Silent oceans: ocean acidification impoverishes natural soundscapes by altering

sound production of the world's noisiest marine invertebrate', *Proceedings of the Royal Society B: Biological Sciences*, no. 283, 2016, 20153046.

8 F. Bertucci, E. Parmentier, G. Lecellier, A. D. Hawkins and D. Lecchini, 'Acoustic indices provide information on the status of coral reefs: an example from Moorea Island in the South Pacific', *Scientific Reports*, no. 6, 2016, 33326.

9 www.globalforestwatch.org

Chapter 24

1 This chapter draws on articles by J. Sueur, 'Le confinement des humains: une trêve sonore pour la nature', *Écho Bruit*, no. 164, 2020, pp. 18–20, and 'Dans le silence du virus: quels effets sur les êtres vivants?', *The Conversation*, 24 March 2020.

2 P.J. Lee and J.H. Jeong, 'Attitudes towards outdoor and neighbour noise during the COVID-19 lockdown, a case study in London', *Sustainable Cities and Societies*, no. 67, 2001, 102768.

3 R.M. Alsina-Pagès, P. Bergadà and C. Martinez-Suquía, 'Changes in the soundscape of Girona during the COVID lockdown', *Journal of the Acoustical Society of America*, no. 149, 2001, pp. 3416–23.

4 P. Munoz, B. Vincent, C. Domergue et al., 'Lockdown during COVID-19 pandemic: impact on road traffic noise and on the perception of sound environment in France', *Noise Mapping*, no. 7, 2020, pp. 287–302.

5 Bruitparif, report 'Effets du confinement puis du déconfinement sur le bruit en Île-de-France', 2020.

6 M. Caniato, F. Bettarello and A. Gasparella, 'Indoor and outdoor noise changes due to the COVID-19 lockdown and their effects on individuals' expectations and preferences', *Scientific Reports*, no. 11, 2021, 16533.

7 *Le Monde*, 8 May 2020. Plantu is a French cartoonist whose work has been a regular feature in *Le Monde* since 1972.

8 E.P. Derryberry, J.N. Phillips, G.E. Derryberry, M.J. Blum and D. Luther, 'Singing in a silent spring: birds respond to a

half-century soundscape reversion during the COVID-19 shutdown', *Science*, no. 370, 2020, pp. 575–9.
9. F. Bertucci, D. Lecchini, C. Greeven et al., 'Changes to an urban marina soundscape associated with COVID-19 lockdown in Guadeloupe', *Environmental Pollution*, no. 289, 2021, 117898.
10. R.M. Rolland, S.E. Parks, K.E. Hunt et al., 'Evidence that ship noise increases stress in right whales', *Proceedings of the Royal Society B: Biological Sciences*, no. 279, 2012, pp. 2363–8.
11. M.K. Pine, L. Wilson, A.G. Jeffs et al., 'A gulf in lockdown: how an enforced ban on recreational vessels increased dolphin and fish communication ranges', *Global Change Biology*, no. 27, 2021, pp. 4839–48.
12. T. Lecocq, S.P. Hicks, K. Van Noten et al., 'Global quieting of high-frequency seismic noise due to COVID-19 pandemic lockdown measures', *Science*, no. 369, 2020, pp. 1338–43.
13. P. Jäggi, 'Listening to reveries: sounds of a post-Anthropocene ecology', *Fusion Journal*, no. 19, 2021, pp. 90–101.

Chapter 25

1. D. Bowler, L. Buyung-Ali, T. Knight and A. Pullin, 'A systematic review of evidence for the added benefits to health of exposure to natural environments', *BMC Public Health*, no. 10, 2010, p. 456.
2. C. Twohig-Bennett and A. Jones, 'The health benefits of the great outdoors: a systematic review and meta-analysis of greenspace exposure and health outcomes', *Environmental Research*, no. 166, 2018, pp. 628–37.
3. E. Ratcliffe, 'Sound and soundscape in restorative natural environments: a narrative literature review', *Environment and Behavior*, no. 36, 2004, pp. 5–31.
4. R.T. Buxton, A.L. Pearson, C. Allou, K. Fristrup and G. Wittemyer, 'A synthesis of health benefits of natural sounds and their distribution in national parks', *Proceedings of the National Academy of Sciences*, no. 118, 2021, 963.

5 B. Mace, P. Bell and R. Loomis, 'Visibility and natural quiet in national parks and wilderness area', *Environment and Behavior*, no. 36, 2004, pp. 5–31.
6 D.M. Ferraro, Z.D. Miller, L.A. Ferguson et al., 'The phantom chorus: birdsong boosts human well-being in protected areas', *Proceedings of the Royal Society B: Biological Sciences*, no. 287, 2020, 20201811.
7 Arrêté préfectoral de protection de biotope; parc naturel régional; zone Natura 2000; zone naturelle d'intérêt écologique, faunistique et floristique.
8 E. Grinfeder, S. Haupert, M. Ducrettet et al., 'Soundscape dynamics of a cold protected forest: dominance of aircraft noise', *Landscape Ecology*, no. 37, 2022, pp. 567–82.
9 R.T. Buxton, M.F. McKenna, D. Mennitt et al., 'Noise pollution is pervasive in U.S. protected areas', *Science*, no. 356, 2017, pp. 521–33.
10 Rapports de l'European Environmental Agency de Copenhague; 'Quiet areas in Europe. The environment unaffected by noise pollution', 2016, and 'Environmental noise in Europe – 2020', 2020.
11 6.4516 square centimetres.
12 N 48.12885°, W 123.68234°.
13 G. Hempton and J. Grossmann, *One Square Inch of Silence: One Man's Quest to Preserve Quiet*, New York: Free Press, 2010.
14 www.quietparks.org
15 www.mountainwilderness.fr